Commercializing Innovation

Providing the inspiration, ideas and knowledge to raise funds, invest in and to commercialize great ideas

Rick McElhinney and Rodney Overton

First published October 2008

Published by Mechpart Publications

Email: publications@mechpart.com
Web: www.mechpart.com
          www.angelsinstitute.com

Copyright 2008 Mechpart Pty Ltd

Cataloguing-in-Publication entry:

McElhinney, Rick and Overton, Rodney

Commercializing Innovation

ISBN 978-0-9804389-2-5

Disclaimer
This material should not be relied upon as a substitute for legal or for other professional advice. No reader should act, or fail to act, on the basis of any of this material as it is for general information only, and so professional advisers should be consulted about any matter contained herein. No warranty is given with respect to the information provided and accordingly, no responsibility for omissions or errors, including responsibility to any person by reason of negligence is accepted by the authors, contributors and editors.

Cover Photo
Cover background: The Rosette Nebula, courtesy of N. Wright and the IPHAS consortium. Constructed from data obtained with the Isaac Newton Telescope, La Palma.

The authors

Rick McElhinney BE(hon), MIEAust, CPEng.
Managing Director of Mechpart and a founding Director of Founders Forum Limited and Angels Institute. He is involved as an equity partner and maintains various levels of involvement in a number of manufacturing and technology companies in China, the United States and Asia Pacific.

The Founders Forum is a not-for-profit organization operating in three states assisting start-up companies meet with investors in a public environment. The Angels Institute is a national network of like-minded individuals who seek to support, invest in and grow carefully selected early-stage investor ready ventures.

Rick has been an active member of the University of Toledo Manufacturing and Technology Advisory Board, and the Society of Manufacturing Engineers, and has been a senior member of the Institute of Engineers, since 1978.

Rodney Overton
Rodney Overton is an international award winning writer (published in four languages) of more than 25 popular *business skills 'how-to'* books covering a wide range of business, human resources, management, planning and sales and marketing topics. He works as business consultant and strategist and has wide experience in facilitating, writing and developing business training courses.

Introduction

If you are an entrepreneur, a mentor or an angel investor looking to succeed with an early-stage venture, this book will provide confidence and enhance your success.

The book is designed to provide inspiration, ideas and knowledge to those who care about the early-stage venture environment. It will provide invaluable insight into what it takes to develop and commercialize innovative ideas.

Many people involved in supporting entrepreneurs believe that it is important to spend time learning about the commercialization process. Books on entrepreneurial activities abound and many target the entrepreneur in an attempt to make them leaders. Entrepreneurs can and do become great leaders; however, most are not skilled sufficiently to take on all the aspects of their future business without assistance. They are often better served by maintaining a focus on their specific expertise.

Can you imagine a major company like Ericsson or Sony making the statement *"Let's give this idea to someone with no commercialization or business experience? We can put them through commercialization and business training programs and let them run with this great idea."*

Unlikely. They would take the idea and surround it with the right team of people with the correct experience and let the ideas person do what they do best without diluting his/her talent. We're not saying people should give away their ideas, we're simply pointing out that success does depend on the team of experts involved in any project.

Good ideas need great people. A team approach is needed to adequately address the multitude of issues that surround any commercialization project. The development of this team is the single biggest challenge facing entrepreneurs, mentors and investors alike.

This book looks into the important elements of commercialization with a focus on supporting all members of a team. It takes the perspective of the investor, understanding that the investor, mentor and entrepreneur are all investors and that all members of the team seek to maximize the return on their investment of time and money.

Investors, mentors and entrepreneurs have a common goal to make their venture a great success. All three need to progress the company through three phases:

1. Make the company attractive for investment
2. Commercialize the product
3. Generate a successful exit.

If you can't prove to an investor that you have a significant opportunity to reach the third goal, you will not and probably should not secure the interest for investment.

The relationship between investors, mentors and entrepreneurs is extremely important. An entrepreneur or mentor will increase their chances of raising the much needed capital for a venture if they understand why and when an investor invests. Getting the investor, mentor and entrepreneur to understand that they are all on the same team and are all investing time or money is not impossible and doing so will increase the chances of success for the venture.

Developing an honest, collaborative approach encouraging transparency will assist in this process.

This book is specifically written for the team to take a venture forward through the process of commercialization for their venture.

It aims to provide information to create wise mentors and make clever investors even better. The book provides a number of templates that make the process easier and more predictable.

Forward (by Dr Rowan Gilmore)

We have a problem. As a country we're not hungry enough, and it's too easy to make money. If not from built property, then from speculating on leases of land where it might be worth digging.

Of course, having a full stomach and money to spend is not something any of us should seek to reverse. But it does make the life of innovators difficult, because prosperous times can mask underlying structural problems that only emerge when times become tough.

San Diego was hungry in the mid-eighties, when the defense industry left town and threw much of its population into the unemployment lines. The city embraced new industries, centered around its university. Today, San Diego is a global center for the wireless industry, home to the mobile phone industry, and the birthplace and playground of much of America's biotechnology industry.

Finland was also a hungry country, in the early nineties, when its traditional Soviet markets disappeared almost overnight. Like San Diego, its population too faced high unemployment. Government and industry leadership decided to pursue a strategy based on technological growth, and the story of Nokia is history. Finland today is characterized by the highest levels of education, research, and collaboration in the world – and has become arguably the most robust economy in Europe.

Innovation is invention followed by commercialization. Organizations like mine – the Australian Institute for Commercialization – welcome this book because it helps to make the commercialization of inventions. Where the venture capital industry fails, angel investors can fill a large gap. Where the management of large companies is lacking in innovation talent, the experience of business mentors and entrepreneurs within small start up companies will reskill it. Where the impatient speculators of stock exchanges demand quarterly results, more far sighted investors can generate more significant returns over time.

This book will help the inventor, the commercializer, or the investor to create real wealth. New businesses need all three – the idea, the business opportunity, and the capital – to succeed. There are solid foundations and help in this book that address all of these.

In the beginning, ingenuity was based on improvisation and grass roots experimentation. Today, we're less hungry, and a bit richer, but we're lucky that people are still willing to give it a go.

Dr. Rowan Gilmore *is CEO of the Institute for Commercialization, a leading service organization helping researchers take their ideas to market.*

Acknowledgements

This book has taken over a year to develop and many people have assisted in the process. Many hard hours by others have resulted in a book that will provide many the opportunity to grow and prosper with their ventures.

Of the many who contributed in the support of this book, acknowledgement needs to be made to the following people:

Adam Blunn	CEO	Australian BioRefining
Adam Gallagher	CEO	Business Growth GC
Andrew Duff	Principal	Venture Positioning Services
Barry Cooper	CEO	Barry Cooper Advisory
Becci Watson	General Manager	The Triton Foundation
Bob Beaumont	COMET Advisor	Beauchamp Pty Ltd
Bob Hayward	Director	KPMG Advisory
Dave Merson	Director	Avand Pty Ltd
Debbie Crowther	CEO	Stratacore International
Dr Jeff Barker	Director	Eduss Broadcast & Media, Inc.
Dr Keith Duncan	Associate Professor	Bond University
Dr Rowan Gilmore	CEO	Australian Institute for Commercialization
Dr Warren Bruce	Director	Bannockburn Superannuation Fund
Graydon Smith	Manager Venture Capital Funds	Ausindustry
Greg Beaver	CEO	Pioneer Development Fund
Ian Mayfield	CEO	GrassAds Pty Ltd
Jay Deeb	Partner	McCullough Robertson
John Bonsib	Retired	
John Mactaggart	Director	Australian Association of Angel Investors
Jordan Green	Partner	Melbourne Venture Partners
Justin Craig	Head	Bond University - Global Strategy, Entrepreneurship and Family Business
Karl Scott	Partner	Gadens Lawyers
Letitia De Lima	Trade Marks Attorney	Visas-R-Us
Geoff McElhinney	Retired	
Mareece McElhinney	Director	The Ladela Growth Fund
Michael Murtagh	COMET Advisor	Cernotech
Neville Sawyer	Chairman	Hunter Founders Forum
Nick Finnie	European Patents	Pizzeys Patent and Trade Mark Attorneys
Noel Lindsay	Professor of Entrepreneurship and Commercialization (ECIC)	The University of Adelaide
Patrick Silvey	Director	VenturePro

Paul Steer	Partner	KPMG
Richard Hayes	Director	RHI Limited
Richard Symon	CEO	National Stock Exchange of Australia
Rick Anstey	Founder/Partner	iQfunds
Russell Barnett	Principal	Australian Venture Consultants
Ryan Glick	Director	Divergent Capital
Scott Standen	Partner	Hynes Lawyers
Stewart Gow	Director	AAAI
Terry McCosker	CEO	Resource Consulting Services
Theo Scherman	CEO	Eduss Broadcast & Media, Inc.
Tony White	CEO	Cheeta International
Viki Forrest	CEO	ANZA Technology Network

A special acknowledgement to:

Hynes Lawyers, in particular Scott Standen for their efforts in developing content for the chapter on shareholders' agreements.

Pizzeys Patent and Trademark Attorneys, in particular Nick Finnie for contributions to the Intellectual Property chapter.

StrataCore International, in particular Debbie Crowther for reviewing financial reporting aspects of the book and for developing the chapter, Understanding Financial Statements.

Contents

1

Entrepreneur Preparation

What is an entrepreneur?

Entrepreneurship is about taking risks, being passionate about the business, continually articulating the vision and recognizing and then maximizing new opportunities.

This chapter is written from the perspective of an entrepreneur before he/she has developed the team or the mentoring team itself in very early preparation of commercializing their idea. Thus we will commence by explaining what an entrepreneur is and what an entrepreneur does.

The very nature of entrepreneurship ensures that some individuals and companies will fail. To grow an entrepreneurial company requires constant adjustments to meet the marketplace and competition.

Entrepreneurship has developed a long way from the 1980s when people asked where all the entrepreneurs were, and expected the response, 'in jail'.

Richard de Cantillon[1] introduced the term 'entrepreneur' in the early 1700's, when he identified risk bearing as the primary role of entrepreneurs. Since then, the definitions of an entrepreneur and of entrepreneurship have evolved in many different and sometimes contradictory ways.

In the 1950s, academic attention shifted from the economic role played by entrepreneurial activity to analysis of the personal characteristics of entrepreneurs. Recently, interest in entrepreneurship has expanded to government, academia and practice.

Working with investors

Angel investors in your ideas want to be able to work with you on a day-to-day basis in a professional manner and without hassles. Investors will always give preference to first ate people and a second rate idea, rather than a first rate idea and second rate people.

---

[1] Richard de Cantillon (1680-1734), Irish banker and economist

J.B. Say[2], an early 19th century French economist is generally credited with recognizing that the entrepreneur in a capitalist society is 'the pivot' on which everything turns.

A more recent definition of an entrepreneur is:
One who reforms or revolutionizes the pattern of production by exploiting an invention or, more generally, an untried technological possibility for producing a new commodity or producing an old one in a new way, by opening up a new source of supply of materials or a new outlet for products by reorganizing an industry.

In traditional economics a basic principle is that economic resources - the means of producing goods and services - are limited or scarce. Economic resources historically are often defined as property resources - land or raw materials and capital - and human resources - labor and entrepreneurial ability. Therefore, entrepreneurial ability is one of the four cornerstones of our economy.

What is meant by entrepreneurial ability? The four key components are essentially:
1. An entrepreneur is the one who takes the initiative to combine land, capital, and labor to produce a good or service in what is hoped will be a profitable venture.
2. An entrepreneur is a person who makes basic business policy decisions that set the course of the business enterprise.
3. An entrepreneur is an innovator - a person who attempts to introduce on a commercial basis new products, new productive techniques, or even new forms of business organization.
4. An entrepreneur is a risk taker, risking not only time, effort and business reputation, but their invested funds and those of associates or stockholders.

The availability of these resources directly affects how robust the economy is. Historically, being entrepreneurial has been outside the mainstream of business. Today, with the internet boom, entrepreneurs have become one of the most dynamic forces in the economy.

Successful entrepreneurs attract the very best people to assist them by offering equity and by selling the vision of their venture. Entrepreneurs who secure a motivated and skilled team gain increased venture value and often accelerate the commercialization process.

The professional entrepreneur

Most entrepreneurs, based on the definitions provided above, exhibit a number of weaknesses and are inexperienced. Some exhibit extraordinary talent and some have remarkable experience which provides the confidence to work through many difficult circumstances.

These "professional entrepreneurs" generally don't fail to succeed. They may change the business plan, redirect product development or change the market approach. Most professional entrepreneurs have been involved in the game for many years and generally get involved in an existing opportunity to support the efforts of others. They are rare and unbelievably valuable. We will do well if we can develop more professional entrepreneurs to support good innovations through the difficult commercialization processes.

---

[2] J. B. Say (1767-1832), the first academic teacher of economics in France

The term entrepreneur is used loosely to encompass the "want-to-be" entrepreneur (the inventor) and the professional entrepreneur. Our challenge as a nation is to develop extraordinary entrepreneurs (professional entrepreneurs) so that there is a sufficient supply to embed these unique individuals when and where needed into existing early-stage opportunities. Being able to recognize the need to be surrounded by good people, including a professional entrepreneur, is a key step in developing entrepreneurial talent.

Making a start on commercializing your innovative idea

Other than the invention or business idea itself, the starting point is when the entrepreneur has a clear definition of what the product, customer and market looks like. We assume that the entrepreneur already has this idea well formed and that it is a commercially viable opportunity. The entrepreneur may not have a complete grasp of all that is needed, but it is assumed that he/she can present the opportunity and explain the potential well. On this assumption, the entrepreneur is ready to develop the team required to take the company to market.

An entrepreneur may take the route of doing it all alone. Generally, there is a period where the entrepreneur must work alone. Doing too much alone can create fundamental problems that waste time and have to be later revisited by others. Doing too little means that the mentors and investors may not see the idea being sufficiently significant for investment of their time or money. The sooner the entrepreneur is able to attract a mentor or investor to the venture the sooner an entrepreneur can accelerate the process.

If your team is serious about turning the business into commercial reality and creating a cash flow and income stream from your ideas, a good starting point is to decide on your business structure and register your business. Your first stop should be the U.S. Small Business Administration's (SBA) Small Business Planner which can be found at **www.sba.gov**. This guide provides information for developing business plans, and steps to take to start and manage a business.

For specific information on registering your business in your state, visit **www.business.gov/states/**.

Once you have registered your business and secured a business name, you will have established the basics for someone who is serious about their commitment to a business enterprise. Your commitment to your idea is important and in many instances critical. You should be able to claim any expenses incurred in commercializing your ideas as a deduction on your income tax. Make sure that you keep a record of all your genuine expenses in your attempts to commercialize your ideas. It is a good idea to use a diary to record all of your meetings in this regard. If you catch a taxi to a meeting for instance, record this in your diary and obtain a receipt so that you have a tangible record of your expenses in order to claim it as a business expense in your taxation return.

Any person or business who may have an interest in buying your ideas or having dealings with your venture will expect you to behave and conduct yourself in a professional, business-like manner. Many ideas people stumble at this first hurdle - they do not present themselves at all well in a business situation. We look at presenting yourself professionally to angels and potential business partners and in meetings in detail later in this book.

As an entrepreneur, have some quality stationery printed - letterheads and business cards - (or create your own on your computer) so that you and your venture present as being serious and professional.

In our recent experience a determined individual was making real progress in commercializing their ideas. However, they were miffed that telephone calls were never answered and that their faxes were never responded to. It turned out their telephone was unattended all day - it had no answering service or paging service. Their faxes had no contact details at all and even the number it was sent from was missing!

It would be nice to think you can run an organisation between nine and five but the reality is, it takes what it takes.

Entrepreneurs should have a detailed resume and be able to present the venture opportunity well. Investors will ask themselves, "*Who are you? What do you have to offer? Why should I become involved with you?*" and most critical of all, "*Why would I give you my money?*"

An important point to keep in mind constantly is that the reason for trying to commercialize any venture is to make a profit including an allowance for profit on your valuable time and effort. There is no joy in 'breaking even' (there is really no such thing), or even worse losing money.

If your venture consistently loses money in attempts to commercialize ideas you will need to rethink the ventures' goals and objectives. Don't forget that you will probably not be able to commercialize your idea in a matter of days. Somewhere between six months and two years is far more realistic.

Always bear in mind that anyone at all, an individual or a multi-national corporation, who is interested in commercializing your idea, will usually be interested for just one basic reason; to make a profit.

There may be other reasons such as extending or complementing an existing product range or keeping competitors at bay and therefore you will need to think through the position of any potential business partner. However, long term if a product or service does not make a profit it will be discarded for one that does. Even worse, of course, if products do not make profits for businesses, the business will eventually and inevitably become insolvent.

In our experience, most - if not all people involved in trying to commercialize their ideas - greatly underestimate the difficulties involved. These people often lack the commercial experience and expertise. They overlook the fact that most commercial organizations have experienced and qualified staff doing exactly what they think they can achieve (often with no commercial experience at all). The same people overlook the myriad of expenses incurred in commercializing a product or service and do not take into account the sometimes extended time required for customers to accept new products or services.

A manufactured product often sells for around six times its cost. You need to add on many extra costs - packaging, marketing, transport, dealer mark-up (much more than most people think), co-operative advertising and general business costs.

For many people there is a major cultural gap to overcome - for instance a fireman with a brilliant idea may not be able to comprehend the work culture of an organization that they will need to work with to ensure commercial viability and success of their idea or product.

Who has the power when attempting to commercialize your idea or product? It will seldom be the ideas person. Who needs whom the most?

Most importantly you will need to prepare a business plan which details how your idea can be turned into a commercial success. The next chapter provides detailed information on Business Planning.

Born global

The development of the commercialization or a product or service often starts with the decision to decide on market location.

Starting a company in your state offers the ability to:
- Create a test market efficiently and inexpensively
- Experiment with a business model and generally to refine it to "get it right" before a venture can take on the larger national and international markets
- Prove concepts and position the business to more readily attract the required funds

Starting in your state can also:
- Drain valuable resources that could be better leveraged nationally
- Slow market acceleration into major markets
- Produce a failure because of the limited market size
- Create a good model for use in your state that does not work in other markets

Sometimes a product simply belongs in a different market than your local market. Most competitors, trade shows, manufacturers, suppliers and alliance do not reside in your state.

The latest trend in venture development is "born global" and these ventures understand that your local market is a small part of the opportunity. Using your local market strategically can be important and needs to be well considered, however, the decision to approach larger markets must be equally considered to develop the winning formulae.

Methods of protecting your idea

The United States Patent and Trademark Office (www.uspto.gov) offers a range of products for the protection of intellectual property (IP). In many instances intellectual property will be of major concern and importance to entrepreneurs. A patent attorney should be consulted rather than trying to arrange protection yourself. You will find them listed in the Yellow Pages™ or on the internet. Whilst it is not always possible to undertake every aspect of IP protection, going through the process will provide the additional benefit of ensuring that you are not infringing on others intellectual property. Please review Chapter 17 "Intellectual Property".

PATENTS protect inventions, that is, a new or improved product or process. Patenting provides protection and control over an invention for up to 20 years.

TRADEMARKS protect words, symbols or pictures, or a combination of these, and they distinguish the goods and services of one trader from those of another.

DOMAIN NAME REGISTRATION Thinking through the potential product and company name should be part of your early brand processing. Doing so later in the process can prove difficult.

DESIGN PATENTS protect artistic and literary works, such as books, paintings and music, but also protect computer programs and engineering drawings (this protection is automatic and does not need to be applied for).

PLANT PATENT protect new plant varieties for a period of 20 years.

TRADE SECRETS protect trade know-how and other confidential information.

Intellectual property can be a valuable asset and should be addressed in the business plan. Intellectual property may require a special strategy of its own to ensure that each element is given the appropriate care and attention. Always remember that once you sell something that you have created, you trigger time limits for application for a patent on the product.

Prior to patent application, strategies may be required to limit the public disclosure of the invention. It is in this early stage effectively a trade secret.

When writing your business plan you should take stock of everything that has been created and is essential to your company. This should include the business name and logo, new ideas, new services, new products, new manufacturing techniques, promotional material, videos and the outcomes of research and development.

Value adding

You should carefully think about value adding to your product or service. For instance car manufacturers use value adding to create a more expensive product by utilizing a basic product. By adding accessories and improved finishes to a basic model they are able to create a more expensive product (and usually a more profitable one). A more expensive value added product must be recognized as more valuable in the eyes of the consumer. When you sell your product, does it makes sense to:
• Sell a maintenance contract
• Sell regular updates of your product
• Sell a warranty
• Extend your range of products regularly

Getting paid

Entrepreneurs sometimes have expectations of making a quick sale of their idea and walking away with a cash windfall. This will probably never be the case as any buyer of your ideas will have all the power in any negotiations.

In our experience it is not unusual for people to have totally unrealistic expectations of million dollar payouts and high royalties based on sales, for a very raw idea that still requires considerable development.

You should carefully consider why anybody would pay you a fee for your idea. The commercialization and marketing of your idea to make it available to consumers and users will involve considerable expense before any profits accrue. In many cases there may never be any profits.

Months or even years later, when they do finalize a sale, they will invariably settle for a commercially realistic amount which may be far less than their initial aspirations.

However, in the case of intellectual property rights, you may be able to sell them at least once to multiple countries. You may also be able to obtain a signing fee, a fee for the option and/or a royalty for each product sold. Royalties can have a finite life.

Sell yourself

Make sure you have an up-to-date resume that highlights your skills, qualifications and experience in developing and selling new ideas. Your potential partners will ask, "*Who are you? What have you done?*" Tell them in your resume.

Why won't my idea or product sell?

Many entrepreneurs and ideas-people are surprised and even downright miffed when their idea will not sell. Many assume if a particular store had their product sitting on the shelf it will automatically sell. Such is never the case of course. Most stores have a merchandising and ranging policy. Their stock must meet certain specific criteria and return a set amount of sales and profits from the amount of space allocated.

Some basic reasons why products or services fail to sell:
- There is no effective market for the product
- The product is not being sold in the right way
- The product is not being sold in the right market
- The product is not competitive in terms of price, quality, or service
- There is 'unfair' competition, possibly because of subsidies or tariffs
- The company has internal weaknesses - thus, costs are too high, productivity is too low, quality control or delivery times are poor, etc.

What else can you do to ensure success with commercializing your ideas?

Always be highly critical of performance - especially your own. Never take your eye off the main objective - especially one you have set yourself. Exactly what do you want to achieve with your idea or product? Set realistic goals and targets.

Success secrets

Fast-growth entrepreneurial companies are a different breed, with their own set of needs and ways of operating. They can reinvent themselves every 12 months, but have three-year strategic plans. They can be "born global" but be highly patriotic and intent on creating jobs. More needs to be done to understand, encourage and assist fast-growth entrepreneurial companies, as contradictions like these can be disconcerting for government, banks and service providers.

Tips for commercializing and selling your products

- Be prepared to give 100 percent commitment (and even more) of your own efforts to make your idea or product successful
- LISTEN. Before you attempt to commercialize your idea, ask potential customers if they would use or buy your product
- Ask how the product or service might be improved
- Find out what potential customers (really) want to buy. In most cases what they want to buy is different from what you want to sell
- Do not assume that your idea or product is a 'good idea'
- Understand the culture and protocol of the industry you want to sell to?

- Be aware of commercial reality. Many people find it hard to accept that a retailer, in most cases will make more profit on a product than the manufacturer
- Realize that it may take months to be paid for your product and there will invariably be bad debts
- The need for an advertising budget and an integrated sales and marketing campaign. Do you understand how sales and marketing in the world of commerce functions? It can take months to obtain a sales appointment with some large organizations. Most products and services have a marketing budget of around five percent of sales
- Understand the apathy of business and the public in general, to change and new products
- Provide for market research and on-going research and development. Research and development involved in most successful new products is in the order of one to three years. Last night's 'good idea' will require lots of development, usually in many stages over a period of time
- Understand the need for products to meet government and industry regulations
- Don't become paranoid about your ideas. This is a common mistake and will hinder your ability to work with people prepared to assist you

Although Fortune 500 companies have lost more than five million jobs since 1980, more than 34 million new jobs have been added to the economy in the same period, the majority created by entrepreneurs and small businesses.

Common pitfalls in commercializing and selling products

- The notion that someone will come along with a handful of money to buy an untried and unproven product
- It is generally the case that a product will retail for three to six times its manufactured cost
- An unwillingness to seek out professional Sales and Marketing advice, which should pay for itself in the money your venture will save in the long term
- Going into production of an unproven product without properly checking manufacturing costs is a common occurrence. People launching new products arrange for 'friends and mates' to make a batch of their product which is inevitably, overpriced. A overpricing factor of 75 percent is not uncommon
- Products do not sell themselves in retail shops. Products require point of sale displays, marketing and advertising
- You have far more interest in selling your product than the retailer. In fact you will have to pull people to the retailer, rather than just push your product to the retailer
- The notion that the USA is a huge market, just waiting for my idea. Consider launching it in your home state first. Some companies indeed are destined for larger markets, however few should attempt to do so at the commencement of commercialization. It can prove advantageous to understand customer reaction on a local basis and to go later armed with increased business and customer experience
- 'If I sell to 10 percent of the population ...... ' Generally unrealistic - 0.5-1.0 percent is a far more practical (and still a difficult) target even for a popular and essential consumer product
- Articulate your vision at every opportunity - many people are paranoid about others finding out about their product, even after it has been patented and is being sold in the market place. Many opportunities are lost at launch stage because of this paranoia - including editorial type stories about new products in the media
- You need absolute commitment and persistence with your product. It is not unusual for ideas-people to take three or four months off work in order to sell their idea or concept. Almost invariably after the first week off work they realize that their planning is inadequate. Who are they going to contact and sell to? To succeed, thorough planning is a requirement

Some critical issues for Entrepreneurs

- The ability to source finance
- Contacts
- Commercial skill
- Management skills
- Technical skills
- Willingness to listen

An exercise - Identifying Key Performance Indicators (KPI's)

1. **Can you identify barriers to entry for the areas of business you intend operating in?**
   For instance, they may be:
   - ☐ Money - large amounts of capital
   - ☐ Large investment in plant
   - ☐ Skilled people
   - ☐ Access to core products
   - ☐ Your ability to take your product or service to the commercialization stage

2. **Can you identify key success factors for your business idea?**
   For instance, they may be:
   - ☐ A distribution network
   - ☐ High levels of service
   - ☐ Brand awareness
   - ☐ Technology

3. **Can you identify KPI's to measure success of your business and industry?**
   For instance, they may be:
   - ☐ Market share
   - ☐ Net and gross profit margins
   - ☐ Return on investment
   - ☐ Distributor agreements
   - ☐ Stock turns

4. **Can you identify KPI's that drive revenues in your business?**
   For instance, they may be:
   - ☐ Advertising volume
   - ☐ Sales call volume
   - ☐ Trade show exposure
   - ☐ Production

24 Tips for Entrepreneurs by Entrepreneurs

Ready to leave your job behind and commence your entrepreneurial business? It takes a certain kind of person to make it through the first few years. To help you along, we have culled the best tips from people with years of entrepreneurship behind them.

1. Don't work for less than what you can afford, but do offer a discount to customers who sign contracts with you
2. Surround yourself with emotionally supportive people and don't be discouraged by anyone. If your idea is good and you are committed to seeing it through the first few tough years, your chance of success is great
3. Be flexible in your thinking. Prepare to change the way you operate, the products you use and the services you offer to fill the demand of your customers
4. Admit your mistakes, correct them and carry on.
5. Develop good relationships with your bankers and creditors. Show a sincere interest in solving problems. Pay as much as you can afford to all creditors to whom you owe money
6. Develop knowledge! Surrounding yourself with great people works very well, however, it is invaluable to be in a position to understand the state of play. You also may need to develop additional skills and knowledge as you wear many hats in the early days and as your position in the company changes over time
7. Avoid complete isolation. Even if you work closely with your clients' in-house staff, you won't be part of a gang anymore. Develop a network of entrepreneurs to see regularly and bounce ideas off, vent and share successes
8. Separate your work and personal lives. Establish a schedule of core, consistent working hours. When you're not available to clients, record a message on your machine letting them know when they can expect a reply. Let them know how to reach you in an emergency
9. Schedule time to think every day. If you fill your date book with activities every second, your business will never grow
10. Schedule time for whatever is your passion at least several times a week - recharge your batteries!
11. Write a business plan so you are clear on what you are doing, and update it every year
12. Be sincere with callers and act quickly to correct any problems.
13. Confirm email orders personally and immediately
14. When you find someone smarter than you, hire them!
15. Solicit advice from knowledgeable people
16. Don't enter a business or a venture that you have no knowledge of. You will be behind the eight-ball the rest of your business life
17. Have an existing, committed client base and start locally
18. Be aware that you will burn through your funding quickly, so ensure you are covered through to at least the second year
19. Focus on a specific goal and take action on it until you get it done
20. Never worry about how to get things done when you are first developing your idea. Money and resources will come together once you know your goal and have taken action
21. Make quality in every aspect of your business your primary focus and aim. If it isn't, you will eventually go out of business

22. Use the Internet. Build a website, have one built, start an email newsletter, buy banner advertisements, join lists and newsgroups
23. Delegate. You might have to hire good outside professionals to ensure you will have money down the road
24. Surround yourself with the best people available wherever possible

In the time of Christopher Columbus, the advisory committee to Ferdinand and Isabella of Spain wrote:

'*So many centuries after the Creation, it is unlikely that anyone could find hitherto unknown lands of any value.*'

What concerns Entrepreneurs?

- Continual development and improvement of the business plan
- My location is not the best to launch a new product from
- Constant difficulties in raising capital
- The need to be a global organization
- The need to develop unique organizational cultures
- Forming strategic alliances
- Developing trust and relationships with clients
- Recruiting high-quality staff and creating a team
- Expanding into new markets
- Learning from mistakes and moving on
- Ensuring regular management meetings
- Constantly monitoring progress with a control mechanism

Amateurism to Entrepreneurism

Tom Richman in *Creators of the New Economy* hypothesizes that what has really occurred is that entrepreneurism has changed dramatically from amateurism to what he terms the professional entrepreneur.

What he is seeing is an evolution in entrepreneurism, not only because motivation from downsizing is putting more talented people out of work, but also because of the opportunities available from globalization and the virtual marketplace. Many very skilled people are joining the entrepreneurial ranks, raising the level of business knowledge and skill.

He distinguishes the following differences between the two:

Amateur Entrepreneur	Professional Entrepreneur
Local	Global
Snap Decisions	Consensus
Heart	Market
Lone Ranger	Networker
Knockoffs	Innovations
Idea	Execution
Knows the Trade	Knows the Business
Secretive	Open
Novice	Veteran
Self-reliant	Inquisitive
Pro-phobe (dislikes professionals)	Pro-phile
Start-up	Start-up or Whatever
Organizationally Orthodox	Organizationally Innovative
Trade Association Member	Web Surfer
Self-sufficient	Virtual
Think Small	Think Big
Small-business Founder	Entrepreneur
Seat-of-the-pants	Business Plan
Boss	Leader
Male	Mixed
Supportive Spouse at Home Spouse	Runs Own Business
Automation	Innovation
Intuition	Education
Research Backwater	Research Mainstream
Price Takers	Value Makers
Personal Financial Plan is the Business	Is Part of Personal Finance Plan
Art	Science
Equity Control	Performance Control
Company	Career

The clear conclusion from all this is that entrepreneurism is a dynamic, developing part of the economy at this time in history. Entrepreneurism itself is emerging and maturing. What it will be as a mature contributor to the economy is yet to be determined, but certainly innovation, knowledge and globalization are important factors.

Are you capable?

Forming your own business or company is not easy and demands enormous commitment and perseverance. If you can answer a majority of the following 30 questions with a distinct 'yes', then it is well worth considering in detail the idea of forming your own company or proceeding with your business project.

1. Am I a leader?
2. Am I ambitious?
3. Do I enjoy learning?
4. Can I evaluate experiences?
5. Do I work on my own initiative?
6. Do I have the courage to dare taking a risk?
7. Can I stand up under defeat and set-backs?
8. Do I have my own ideas?
9. Can I make these ideas understandable to others?
10. Can I work persistently towards a goal?
11. Can I negotiate skillfully?
12. Do I succeed in making contact quickly?
13. Do I enjoy achieving more than the others?
14. Can I manage people well?
15. Do I trust other people?
16. Do I understand and sympathize with others' mistakes?
17. Can I praise, or even more, reproach someone without offending them?
18. Do I have a good memory?
19. Do I have sufficient education?
20. Can I plan long term?
21. Am I intellectually active?
22. Am I critical of myself?
23. Am I in good enough physical condition to take on additional burdens?
24. Do I have my finances under control?
25. Do I have a healthy financial basis at my disposition?
26. Do my family and friends believe in what I'm doing?
27. Am I prepared to give up leisure time, hobbies and vacation?
28. Is it my own desire to become self-employed?
29. Am I capable of being enthusiastic?
30. Do I maintain perspective in stressful situations?

If you can answer more than half of these questions with 'yes', then you can consider planning and forming a company. But remember; a company founder must be capable of overcoming numerous hurdles and solving innumerable problems. Much can be solved by building skilled and experienced people around you to undertake the many tasks required.

Source: KMU Foundation, Switzerland

Building a team

Once you have completed the basics and are ready to move forward as a true entrepreneur, you are now ready to develop your team. One of the most important things needed when commercializing an idea is to attract and develop a team of people or contract advisors who can assist you to achieve your goals and targets and to provide advice on a range of issues.

Building and developing a team of people is a very difficult task at any time. It is an even more difficult task to build and develop a team as you attempt to commercialize your own idea, usually with a lack of sufficient funds. Of course, you will also need to motivate and reward your team!

In our experience it is not unusual for the ideas-person to try and do everything themselves in an attempt to save money. The ideas-person attempts to write and register the patent themselves. They endeavor to manufacture the product themselves. They endeavor to advertise, sell and market the product or service themselves.

... a team member ... held shares that were worth more than a million dollars on the day of the IPO.

You should identify the extra skills that you need to commercialize your idea. The initial skill for many people is assistance with their intellectual property, which in many cases drains all of their funds. Some other required skills are raising money, production, marketing, packaging, promotion, transport, logistics, advertising and sales.

In hindsight, it is interesting to observe that almost inevitably the ideas that progress to an Initial Public Offering (IPO) on the Stock Exchange - often with great financial rewards - have a team of (very often, high profile) people behind them providing a range of specialist services.

Many if not most ideas-people would state the obvious and claim that they cannot afford to pay for a team of people. An important element of being entrepreneurial and achieving commercial success with your idea is to convince a team of people to work with you. If you cannot afford to pay them, as an entrepreneur you need to come up with other ways to get them on your team. You may not need to employ people on a full time basis. There are many contractors who provide a range of financial, sales and marketing services.

Many ideas-people offer shares in their company in lieu of immediate payment. As we explain later, you need to be investment ready if you want to work on this basis.

However many successful ideas have proceeded to the IPO stage with a specialist team taking their deferred payment in shares which they can sell after the IPO. In one recent case a team member who had worked for nothing up until that stage held shares that were worth more than a $1 million on the day of the IPO.

Getting started - a summary

- Think through which business structure is best for your venture and register your business. With a business established you should be able to claim any tax benefits as you commercialize your ideas.
- You should establish your bona fides as someone who is serious about their commitment to a business enterprise.
- Work with quality letterheads and other business stationery, including business cards.
- Prepare a resume for yourself - tell potential buyers of your ideas about your skills, qualifications and experience.
- You should also be able to claim any expenses incurred in commercializing your ideas as a deduction on your income tax.
- Make sure that you keep records of all your genuine expenses in your attempts to commercialize your ideas.
- Buy a diary to record all of your meetings in this regard.
- A patent attorney can help you protect and register your intellectual property.
- **An important point to keep constantly in mind is that the reason for your trying to commercialize your ideas is to make a profit.** There is no joy in 'breaking even' (there is really no such thing), or even worse losing money. If you consistently lose money in your attempts to commercialize your ideas you will need to rethink your goals and objectives.
- Always bear in mind that anyone at all - be it an individual, or at the other end of the scale a multi-national corporation - who is interested in commercializing your idea, will be interested for just one basic reason; to make a profit. There may be other secondary reasons such as extending or complementing an existing product range or keeping competitors at bay, but even then they want to make a profit!
- However, long term, if a product or service does not make a profit it will be discarded for one that does. Even worse of course if products do not make profits for businesses, the business will eventually and inevitably become insolvent.
- Build and develop your team of people and advisors with specialist skills to assist in commercializing your idea. Surround yourself with the very best people you can attract to your venture.
- **Keep on asking yourself - who are those with a beneficial interest in my product? Identify them and talk to them about your ideas.**

2

Planning for Commercialization

Planning to successfully commercialize your idea should involve a number of planning steps. The preparation of a business plan is virtually a mandatory requirement for the entrepreneur in order to develop and further the commercialization of their idea.

Conversely, it is a virtual given that potential funders including angels and venture capitalists will ask to see the business plan before meeting with you.

Developing a business plan will force you to think through some important issues that you may not otherwise consider - a beneficial process. Your plan will become a valuable tool as you set out to raise money for your business and it will provide milestones in your control process to gauge your success by measuring results against aims and objectives.

A business plan should be much more than a collection of financial statements and cash flow projections. The business plan should tell the person reading it how you are going to obtain strong results including sustained growth and profits, loyal customers and a high performing workforce.

To do this, your business plan will need to address many elements of the business especially sales and marketing as well as people (human resources), processes, customers (forming relationships), business strategies, goal setting, brand building, leadership and finance. Your business plan should address how your business intends creating a distinct and profitable niche in its market place utilizing your unique selling proposition.

A favorite topic of ours in regard to business planning is how some 'business professionals' place huge emphasis on a budget and the associated cash flow as a key element of their business plan preparation while completely ignoring how the business will actually create these budgeted cash flows. These 'business professionals' apparently do not understand (and have no knowledge of) people, processes, customers, business strategies, sales, marketing, brand building and leadership.

A business plan should be a dynamic document and not sit on the shelf after it has been finalized. Many people fall into the trap of preparing a business plan and after some initial use and reference to it, the business plan is filed away and never referred to again. Your business plan should be constantly referred to and constantly updated, taking into account market forces and the constant change involved in most industries.

And remember, a business plan should be like a laser - not a shotgun and someone needs to be responsible for driving the business plan.

A business plan is essential when planning to commercialize and launch new products or services. The business plan should tell the person reading it:

- What is planned
- Who will do it
- When it will be done
- How much it will cost

WHAT, WHO, WHEN, HOW, are key words in all planning decisions.

Planning framework. Business Planning is a process and can be broken down into steps:

- Establish objectives
- Develop basic assumptions or premises
- Identify alternative courses of action
- Evaluate alternative courses of action
- Implement the plan

Writing a business plan to appeal to investors

Any business plan pitched at potential investors must:

- Explain why there is a market for the product or service.
- Describe the core technology and its competitive advantage.
- Explain how the product or service will be mass produced.
- Detail how the product or service will be marketed, distributed and sold.
- Explain how sales targets will be reached.
- Detail the experience, skills and qualifications of senior management.
- Detail how the company's intellectual property will be protected.
- Identify key milestones to be achieved, by item, time, cost and the person responsible.
- Identify key risks and how those risks have been addressed.
- Provide a one or two page executive summary.

The business planning process

A business plan is a requirement for all types of organizations - manufacturing, wholesale, service, non-profit, charity, government, etc.

Business planning can prove to be a valuable process. It is undeniably hard work but ultimately exceptionally rewarding. It will cleanse and refocus your thinking about business and thus help you develop your approach to it. In undertaking Business Planning you will learn a lot more about your business and thus acquire more confidence in how to manage it.

Many business plans are completed by unskilled entrepreneurs who repeat various content items under different headings. For example, in the marketing section, rather than defining the size and key elements of the market, they repeat information relating to sales strategies or projections. Unfortunately, seasoned investors often pass over such documents with the belief that if the team can't understand key elements of a business plan, they'll probably not be great at developing a business.

Without a business plan you can only react to events, and as such your achievements will be limited. A business plan helps you focus on the future and will assist in identifying a clear course of action to lead you there.

The thinking process is quite straightforward. It starts with the conceptualization of a vision and then moves through an iterative cycle of review and analysis to the establishment of strategic priority objectives supported by detailed projections. The iterative cycle is simply a matter of analyzing and clarifying your projections for the future and, to ensure feasibility, comparing these with an analysis of the current situation and recent performance.

Before you embark on the process of preparing a business plan you need to determine the purpose of the plan and who it is aimed at and being written for. It may be for yourself, your team with the object of making the business perform better, the bank manager, a backer or investor, or a combination of these.

How long should a business plan be?

As a general rule, a good plan will probably comprise around 50 detailed pages, plus financial statements and appendices. However many plans comprise just a few succinct pages. Many investors prefer a plan of around 20 to 25 pages, some banks require only five to 10 pages of mainly financial projections, while many plans run to over 100 pages.

How long will it take to write a good business plan?

In our experience, to write a business plan can take as little as one or two weeks - or in other cases up to six months. Gathering and researching appropriate data and benchmarking competitors and other comparable industries is important and can take considerable time.

Business planning stages

1. **The reasons and the purpose of this Business Plan**. Start by defining the reasons you are writing the business plan and the purposes you will use the plan for.
2. **Situation analysis.** This involves analyzing exactly where the business or organization is currently, and defining the mission, goals, targets and objectives.
3. **Action Plan.** This involves defining exactly how and when you intend achieving your goals and objectives, and delegating personnel responsible for the process.
4. **Implementation - follow up.** A critical and important stage in the business planning process. And don't forget that any business plan should be reviewed and updated on a regular basis.

A willingness to listen

Mark Casson's[3] definition of the entrepreneur emphasizes the importance of information in decision making. The entrepreneur's ability to gain access to relevant information when business planning provides the competitive edge needed for entrepreneurial success. As managers, entrepreneurs provide three functions:

1. Strategic planning arising from the development of ideas based on foresight and knowledge of the market place.
2. Leadership of people both within and external to the organizations, where leadership is defined as the ability to influence people to achieve objectives.
3. Administrative, organizational, analytical and delegation abilities ensuring the effective administration of the entrepreneurial unit throughout the management-based systems.

Planning for success

Some essential issues for survival in your Business
1. **Your personal aims.** How do you want your life to be?
2. **Your strategic objective.** A very clear statement of what your business has to do to achieve your personal aims.
3. **Your organizational strategy** Organize around functions - not personalities. Plan for the mature business. That is: Managing Director, Financial Controller, Marketing Manager, etc.
4. **Your management strategy.** The system or process by which management decisions are made. That is an automatic system, not a routine.
5. **Your people strategy.** Create an environment where people will want to do what you want.
6. **Your marketing strategy.** What your customer wants is really what matters.
7. **Your systems strategy.** The glue that holds your prototype together.

Some business planning goals - steps in the process

By testing a business opportunity against each of these steps, the owner/manager can gain a better grasp of the reality of successfully executing a business opportunity.
1. **Desires or needs**. Goals should be determined based upon what the company or the person desires or needs.
2. **Belief**. Management of the company must believe they can achieve the goal. This must be based on a realistic assessment, yet the goal must make one stretch.
3. **Write it down**. Goals must be written and rewritten in as much detail as possible. Writing it down crystallizes it, creates a memory impression, and makes it clear.
4. **How you will benefit**. Write down the benefits for each goal. This includes noting the differences that will result from achieving the goal. The more reasons the better.
5. **Analyze the current position**, in relation to the individual goals. How much money are you making now? Is there room in the market for another similar product?

---

[3] Professor Mark Casson, economics, University of Reading

6. **Set deadlines**, using the latest outside date. Setting deadlines helps make goal attainment measurable. Deadlines set direction, keep you moving, and help monitor success.

7. **Identify obstacles**. Draw up a list of identifiable obstacles to job attainment. Large obstacles tend to become smaller when written down. When identifying obstacles, high standards should be set - this increases concentration, and, at a minimum, you will at least hit an identifiable goal.

8. **Identify knowledge**. It doesn't matter if it is a personal or a company goal, there is always additional knowledge that must be acquired. You will have to learn something or add to the team someone who has the knowledge.

9. **Identify people**. For both personal or business, people, groups, and their co-operation are needed to obtain goals. Three laws apply:
   a. *The law of return*. Whatever you sow, so shall you reap. You must put in or give before you receive.
   b. *The law of compensation*. Every action has a reaction. Determine what you can provide most effectively.
   c. *The law of service*. You can only achieve by serving or filling a need. Today in business it is called customer service. Go the extra mile; do more than you are paid for.

10. **Make a plan of the last three steps** (7, 8 and 9) and then itemize, prioritize, and list the activities. Review, rewrite, revise; do this as you go along. It is called thinking on paper.

11. **Get a clear mental picture**. You do this as if your goal is already in existence. By doing this visualization, you can achieve the goal to the degree of seeing the details. Remember, the more you can concentrate your gaze on a distant goal, the more apt you are to stumble over something right under your feet. Visualizing in detail helps prevent stumbling.

12. **Back up goal setting with determination**. With all goals, they must be backed with the determination and resolve to never, never give up. Persistence counts. Realistically, there will be setbacks and failures, but these are signs to alter the goal-achieving strategy. Pick yourself up and go on. Keep on going on!

The turn-offs

In general, when do investors start losing interest in a business plan?
When they see or are confronted by:

- Some investors are turned off if a business plan is longer than 25 pages
- An executive summary that is longer than two pages
- 10 pages about the product or service followed by one paragraph about how it will be sold
- No month-by-month cash-flow statement
- No change in expenses when sales increase
- No mention of the company's initial customers

Note: Every investor will want something different from the document. It is very difficult to please all but it remains important to cater for the majority.

A business plan format

(courtesy of Sydney Business Center)

The outline shown here is a useful format to follow if you need to prepare and write a detailed business plan. Angels would inevitably expect you to have a viable business plan in place.

1. **Executive Summary**
   - ☐ You need to capture the interest of your prospective investor
   - ☐ Include an overview of:
     - a. customer value
     - b. the product or service
     - c. target markets
     - d. critical management skills
     - e. what returns are expected?
   - ☐ Clearly state the funding requirements - the offer
   - ☐ The summary should be readable and understandable in around 10 minutes.

2. **The Company**
   - ☐ Explain the company and what it intends to do
   - ☐ Articulate your Mission Statement
   - ☐ State the medium and long term aims and objectives
   - ☐ Describe the key success variables
   - ☐ Highlight the milestones for the next year.

3. **Product or Service**
   - ☐ Define the product or service
   - ☐ Demonstrate the customer value proposition
   - ☐ Discuss the current stage of development
   - ☐ Explain the production processes and needs.

4. **Management Team and Key People**
   - ☐ Describe your management team in detail - their qualifications, skills and experience which are important to, and relate to this business plan
   - ☐ Explain how responsibilities will be delegated
   - ☐ Indicate any positions which are yet to be filled
   - ☐ List your key advisors.

5. **The Market**
   - ☐ Describe your customers - the demographics
   - ☐ Define the target markets - their size and their current and potential growth
   - ☐ Analyze your competition - their strengths, weaknesses and competitive advantage

6. **Marketing**
   - ☐ Detail how the product or service will be sold
   - ☐ Set out your Marketing Plan
   - ☐ Explain the pricing strategy

7. **Risks**
   - ☐ Define the legal, regulatory, economic and technological risks
   - ☐ Explain how these risks will be addressed

8. **Financial Forecast**
   - ☐ Detail investor returns
   - ☐ Include income forecasts and cash flow statements
   - ☐ Explain your financial assumptions
   - ☐ Outline funding requirements and how the funds will be used.

Appendices The Appendices should contain relevant material which supports the business plan.

How much money will you need?

Many people are not really sure how much money they will require from their potential investor or angel, and there are many who do know and are afraid to ask for the full amount required.

A professional and business-like approach to this perhaps delicate subject, is to prepare a detailed and itemized list showing how you plan to use the money provided by your investor or angel.

You could prepare a simple list based on the example below and include it in your business plan and investment proposal.

ITEM	$ $ $
• Marketing costs	_____
• Sales costs (including wages)	_____
• Management and admin wages	_____
• Research & development (including wages)	_____
• Business infrastructure	_____
• Working capital requirements excluding the above	_____
• Capital works	_____
• Protection of Intellectual Property Rights (IPR's)	_____
• Others	_____
• _____	_____
• _____	_____
• **TOTAL**	_____

SWOT Analysis

Strengths, Weaknesses, Opportunities, Threats

As part of the business planning process an analysis and assessment of the organization's **Strengths, Weaknesses, Opportunities and Threats** (SWOT) should be undertaken. This can assist management in identifying the organization's distinctive competence, skills, culture and resources. Below are some things that a SWOT analysis might say about a retail furniture shop.

STRENGTHS	WEAKNESSES
• Excellent high exposure main road, near city location • Established in same location 10 years • Good cash flow business • Good return on owners funds • Specialist expertise in small, limited, product range • High levels of stock rotation • Deposits provide working capital • Strong consumer base in area	• No other complementary businesses close by • Limited parking • Accessible from one side of street only • No goals or targets • Building looks tired • Showroom needs new image • Sales staff lack motivation • Poor sales facilities in store • No sales contact point in store • Concentrated product range • No 'add on' business and sales • No leadership or motivation • No advertising or marketing plans
MAINTAINING THESE STRENGTHS *What should we do to maintain these strengths?*	*OVERCOMING THESE WEAKNESSES* *What can we do to overcome these weaknesses?*
OPPORTUNITIES	THREATS
• To revamp existing premises and improved image • To increase product range and mix • To motivate and train sales staff • To take on new dealerships • To form strategic alliances	• Many major national furniture create a new retailers within 3 mile radius • Increased parking restrictions • Increased competitor activity in area
TAKING ADVANTAGE OF THESE OPPORTUNITIES *What can I do to take advantage of opportunities?*	*OVERCOMING THESE THREATS* *What can I do to overcome these threats?*

SWOT Analysis
Strengths, Weaknesses, Opportunities, Threats

An exercise - write a SWOT analysis for your own business (an angel may do the same when evaluating your business) - see the previous page for some prompts.

STRENGTHS	WEAKNESSES
MAINTAINING THESE STRENGTHS *What should we do to maintain these strengths?*	***OVERCOMING THESE WEAKNESSES*** *What can we do to overcome these weaknesses?*
OPPORTUNITIES	**THREATS**
TAKING ADVANTAGE OF THESE OPPORTUNITIES *What can I do to take advantage of opportunities?*	***OVERCOMING THESE THREATS*** *What can I do to overcome these threats?*

Winning with new products

- Expect to reduce costs eight to nine percent each year
- Be fast to market (seven months average)
- Expect to have a second generation within two years
- Improve value within two years
- Listen to customers
- Listen to your sales force
- Respond quickly
- Have your product approved by opinion leaders and reviewers
- Look for approval from standards bodies

LUCK

Luck often comes down to being in the right place at the right time. Others claim luck is where preparation and opportunity meet. However to be in the right place at the right time the individual has most certainly done something to be there.
Luck can be broken down into the mnemonic:

L Labor

U Under

C Correct

K Knowledge

Launching a New Product

Try this simple test - rate each item x /10

	Score
• GROWTH RATE / POTENTIAL	_____
• BARRIERS TO ENTRY	_____
• COMPETITOR RIVALRY	_____
• BUYER POWER	_____
• SUPPLIER POWER	_____
• SUBSTITUTES	_____
• YOUR PERSONAL SKILLS	_____
• Add, then calculate a percent	_____

Try it on a:
- sports store
- new car franchise
- liquor store
- your new product or pet project

Unique Selling Point (USP)

**Does your business or product have a USP?
Can you come up with one for it?**

Another quick and easy three point guide and checklist to apply to any new business, product, service or idea you are contemplating becoming involved in is:

IS IT ?   1. A growth market
            2. The correct product
            3. A vehicle for sales
Compare your product against this checklist.

Try other products against this list, such as:
- A new cigarette brand
- What if marijuana were legalized tomorrow?
- An inexpensive imported motor car
- On-site caravans
- A kitchen manufacturing business
- Typewriters
- Computer furniture
- Computer technology

Formulating Strategy

Does your business have a strategic plan? What are the strategies you use to win market share and make profits?

Potential investors and angels will be certain to ask anybody seeking investment for their business what their strategies are.

The aim of strategy is to develop a successful organization, which in most cases means beating your competitors. This entails developing better resources which are more suited to customers' needs in areas including physical, technological, people, financial products or services.

This involves the organization adding more value to its resources than its competitors do and avoiding its competitors catching up, ***to gain a sustainable competitive advantage.***

Strategy is the art of creating value. It provides the intellectual frameworks, conceptual models, and governing ideas that allow a company's managers to identify opportunities for bringing value to customers and for delivering that value at a profit. In this respect, strategy is the way a company defines its business and links together the only two resources that really matter in today's economy; knowledge and relationships or an organization's competencies and customers.

Strategic planning is the process of developing and maintaining a strategic fit between the organization's goals and capabilities and its changing marketing opportunities. It relies on developing a clear company mission, supporting objectives, a sound business portfolio, and coordinated functional strategies.

Corporate level strategy seeks to determine what set of businesses the organization should be in.
Business level strategy is concerned with how the organization should compete in each of its businesses.

Functional level strategy is concerned with how functional departments can support the business level strategy.

Strategic planning relates to creating and maintaining the organization's competitive advantage, which is the basis of its survival in the marketplace. It is broad in scope, has a long term perspective (at least a year for small organizations) and is more concerned with external rather than internal (operating) issues.

> *... strategy is the way a company defines its business and links together the only two resources that really matter in today's economy; knowledge and relationships or an organisation's competencies and customers.*

Specific strategy development involves:

- Setting objectives
- Determining the organization's thrust in the marketplace - its product service mix
- Identifying its target markets and market opportunities.
- Assessing the organization's strengths, weaknesses, opportunities and threats
- Deciding how, in which direction, and how fast the organization should grow
- Deciding what resources will be required
- Evaluating location
- Forecasting future environmental factors likely to enhance or threaten the organization's survival capacity
- No company can control the environmental changes occurring in other businesses and external to their own business. It surrounds them, yet requires that we all adjust our businesses accordingly. The best thing therefore is to plan
- If you shoot from the hip, you may get it right 50 percent of the time
- If you take aim at a specific target, however, you can hit that target every time - that is what most consider the difference between haphazard planning and a business plan

All companies and organizations should have a written strategic business plan and certainly will possess a basic strategy which defines the business it is in, and how it will compete in the market place.

Strategy will be revealed by the decisions and actions a company takes. In many cases the intended strategy will be different from the revealed strategy.

Strategy has four aspects:
1. It is about long term impacts of important choices in relation to resource allocation and business focus
2. It is about decision making
3. It is about the integration and focus of business functions
4. It is about implementation of the decisions

Strategic decisions are characterized by being; important, not easily reversible and with the involvement of the commitment of resources for a significant period of time.

An exercise - Formulating Strategy
1. Identify barriers to entry for your business
2. Identify key success factors for your business
3. Identify key indicators to measure success in your business and industry

Check your strategic planning against the following strategy issues:
1. **Mission** Description, attitude, growth, direction
2. **Objectives** The ambitions of the organization, performance targets
3. **Strategy** Use of resources, competitive advantage, product design, etc.
4. **Tactics** Action, competing in the market place

As part of the setting of strategies you will probably have to address issues such as: What business are we really in? How will we compete and win market share in this business, (and make a profit)? What means will we use to implement our strategy?

Resources

The **Resource-Based View (RBV)** is an economic tool used to determine the strategic resources available to a firm. The fundamental principle of the RBV is that the basis for a competitive advantage of a firm lies primarily in the application of the bundle of valuable resources at the firm's disposal. To transform a short-run competitive advantage into a sustained competitive advantage requires that these resources are heterogeneous in nature and not perfectly mobile. Effectively, this translates into valuable resources that are neither perfectly imitatable nor substitutable without great effort. If these conditions hold, the firm's bundle of resources can assist the firm sustaining above average returns.

A resource checklist

According to the resource advantage theory, **resource-based view (RBV)**, there are three types of resources:
1. **Physical**, such as plant, location and access to raw materials
2. **Human**, such as skills, knowledge and ability
3. **Organizational**, such as culture, structure, procedures and systems

For a resource to be useful in developing a sustainable competitive advantage, it must meet four criteria:
1. The resource must be valuable
2. The resource must be rare
3. There must not be a substitute for the resource
4. The resource must be difficult to imitate

Examples of resources that meet these criteria include the service culture in legendary organizations such as the United States department-store group Nordstrom's, the remarkable level of employee commitment in organizations such as Southwest Airlines, and the mass-customization capabilities of the Dell Computer Corporation.

- ✓ **15 percent of the world's population provides 98 percent of the world's technology innovations.**
- ✓ **Half the world's population is able to adapt these technologies in production and consumption.**
- ✓ **The remaining third is technologically disconnected.**

Jeffrey Sachs, economist

Identifying internal and external resources

1. A business manager or entrepreneur should review the business objectively, as if a third party, and try and identify all of the assets and positive attributes of the business.
2. You should consider what resources the business proprietor or entrepreneur possesses or has access to.
3. What resources can you effectively demonstrate to a potential investor?
4. What resources do you have which a potential investor will be able to measure and quantify?

Internal resources

Internal expertise - the unique technical skills of you and your staff.
- **Time** - are you maximizing your time? What hours does your business trade?
- Money - are you maximizing your debtors and creditors as well as your cash position?
- Are your accounts up to date? Do they reflect a true record of your company?
- **People** - Many people argue that people are the ultimate resource - are you utilizing your people to their full capabilities? Do they (really) understand your business and where you want it to go?
- Can they grow with and support your business?
- Are your people the best in your industry?
- **Plant -** Is there excess capacity? Is there adequate capacity?
- **Intellect** - Can you as the business proprietor demonstrate superior intellect which will assist in convincing investors?
- **Intellectual property -** What patents, copyrights, licenses, etc., do you own?
- **Technology -** Can you demonstrate or supply technology that is at the cutting edge for your industry?

External resources

External expertise. Do you have external providers of unique services who can be classed as a resource for your business?

- Your customers? Customers who will act as advocates for your business?
- Contracts (regular or large) with customers? Contracts with government?
- Your advertising agency?
- Your accountant? Your designer? Your consultant? Your mentor?
- Government agencies?
- Media contacts?
- Formal and informal business networks?
- Who will champion your cause?
- Others?

Selling to and reaching the market place

How can you get your fabulous new idea to the market place?
Selling/commercialization is a major hurdle facing most people with a new concept or idea.

In the week of writing this we were approached by two partners, who after some two years and much expense and heartache had sold only seven of their products. They had registered worldwide patents, and taken and relied on poor and totally unsuitable advice from accountants who had never before been involved in new product development.

A business and marketing plan prepared by their accountants failed to set any goals or targets to address driving business growth and national sales of the product.

Some alternatives which these people could use to drive and grow their product in the market place could include:

1. **Market and sell it yourself** - as the partners had no capital and lacked manufacturing facilities this was not an option.
2. **Call for Expressions of Interest** - don't be frightened to spend money on a large advertisement in a major newspaper, probably around $1,000 to reach the right people and to convey the right image. This could generate enquiries from a range of people and organizations with sufficient funds and ability to drive the product.
3. **Sell the entire concept** - to a major company already operating in the industry with existing trade contacts.
4. **Take on a partner with the ability to provide finance** - always difficult and most people in this situation have problems 'giving' away equity for money. Very few partnerships succeed anyway!
5. **License the concept** - difficult because of the very few sales to date and therefore lack of proof of concept.
6. **Franchise the concept** - difficult to franchise an unproven concept.
7. **Use a manufacturers' agent or trade broker** to sell the product - a very slow, but steady and cost effective way of gaining market share.

Case studies - commercializing Innovation

We are all familiar with the uses of aluminum and accept it as an everyday commodity. Without it many of the things we take for granted and use every day would not exist in their present form.

However aluminum is a fairly recent metal, compared to some such as copper, bronze and iron. A story has it that in the USA in 1883 Charles Martin Hall was in a class when his lecturer Professor Frank F. Jewett spoke about aluminum and the difficulty involved in making it economically viable. Jewitt said, "Any person who discovers a process by which aluminum can be made on a commercial scale will bless humanity and make a fortune for himself."

Hall decided to take up the challenge. To succeed he had to come up with the correct formula and build his own equipment. Professor Jewett acted as mentor and provided facilities, material and knowledge.

After three years Hall produced goblets of aluminum metal by electrolysis of aluminum oxide dissolved in a cryolite-aluminum fluoride mixture. It was, for its time, close to a miracle of chemistry. Hall had beaten the scientific odds and the potential rewards for doing so were his.

Hall then formed the Pittsburgh Reduction Company, the predecessor to Alcoa. Before he could claim financial success, he had to overcome the defection of two backers as well as an attempt by another company to suppress his new process by buying him out. He also had to withstand a challenge to his patent rights by a French scientist who had filed a patent for a similar process.

Hall won all of these battles and his invention is now responsible for many of the major advances since, such as flight.

Orbital Engines

Ralph Sarich is a well known and successful entrepreneur. When he won the Inventor of the Year award in 1972 with his Orbital Engine concept he received huge publicity. In the next year he formed a 50/50 joint venture with Broken Hill Proprietary (BHP) to develop a rotary-style engine.

Between 1986 and 1989 licensing agreements were entered into with Outboard Marine, Ford, General Motors and Mercury Marine. In 1991 the company listed on the New York Stock Exchange. Its share price peaked at around $5 in the early 1990s.

Twenty years later after winning the ABC Inventor of the Year award, Sarich retired from the company and sold most of his share holding.

It was not until 1996, after Sarich had retired from the company, that Mercury Marine launched the first product incorporating the technology that made Sarich wealthy and famous.

This story illustrates what a long and hard road ultimate success can involve.

Returning $100 million on $300,000

WOTIF.com made an astounding success in 2006 with their listing on the Stock Exchange. Launched in 2000, when the tech crash was at its peak, a group of clever investors identified an opportunity and went for it.

Kevin Fitzpatrick a part-time manager, accountant Andrew Brice and rural property manager Lyn Brazil invested in the WOTIF concept and within three years secured in excess of $100 million from the float of WOTIF while retaining over 25 percent of ownership in the company. This is the kind of investment return angel investors are seeking. WOTIF was trading at a capital value of over a billion dollars in early 2008 which placed an additional $250 million in value in the hands of these investors.

These three investors saw value in an opportunity well before others did. Is your venture capable of similar returns?

Instead of buying and reading a newspaper to find a job, why not do it on the internet. Or for employers, save money on expensive newspaper advertising and lodge your advertisement directly on to a website. This concept has delivered a worth of around $130 million to 39 year old **Matthew Rockman.**

SEEK, a large digital media company, the online recruitment firm he founded in 1998 with the two Bassat brothers listed in April 2005. Since listing the share price has increased in value by around four times. In the last reporting year SEEK reported sales of $157 million, a 47 percent increase in job ads and profits of $55 million; an incredible profit margin, matched by very few companies.

Paul Bassat, 39, co-founder of SEEK and its chief executive is reputed to have accumulated a fortune of almost $100 million from SEEK. He is developing a learning division that offers distance and classroom courses in business topics that can be accessed on the SEEK site.

The secret to their success according to Bassat was to identify a great market opportunity and go after it in a focused and disciplined way.

Summary

- A business plan is essential when you are planning to launch new products or services. It should tell the person reading it, what is planned, who will do it, when it will be done, and how much it will cost.
- Many entrepreneurs write a business plan only when they require money, rather than before the business commenced. A good, detailed, business plan can assist in raising substantial sums of money. Make sure your plan stands out from the rest - some 90 percent of business plans sent to investors are thrown away.
- **What, Who, How, Why**, are key words in all planning decisions.
- Plan your goals and objectives - both personal and business and regularly review your goals.
- Be aware of the critical issues in commercializing and launching new ideas and products. Be aware of what you need to do to win with new ideas and products. Be aware of what consumers really want.
- Calling for Registrations of Interest is a cost effective way of identifying interested parties.
- Formulate your strategies for success. Identify internal and external resources. Plan how much money you will need. Prepare a SWOT analysis.
- Be aware of the impression you create - your premises, stationery and your appearance.
- Identify potential problem areas. Ask yourself, "Am I capable?"
- The first few pages of your business plan are critical, especially the executive summary - they must attract and hold the readers interest.
- Your technology is not as important to investors as the potential returns. Tell the investors what returns they can expect on their investment.
- Accountants write business plans for banks which use automated risk analysis - for rapid growth situations this type of plan will seldom appeal. The entrepreneur did not write the plan and will have problems articulating the plan. Tell the reader how you intend achieving economies of scale in your

rapidly expanding business. If you have to double overheads to double sales, you have a problem.

- Many organizations who are not currently competitors have the capabilities to become future competitors when they identify attractive niche markets.
- Tell the reader of your plan about your sustainable competitive advantage. Tell the reader of your plan about the strengths of your business, your distribution, sales force, financial strengths, intellectual property, potential market and its strengths to support it against competition.

A consensus of advice from entrepreneurs

- **Research your market, but do not take too long to act.**
- **Start your business when you have a customer.**
- **Try your new venture as a side line first.**
- **Plan your objectives within specific time frames.**
- **Surround yourself with people smarter than yourself.**
- **Do not be afraid to fail.**
- **Use a good accountant / advisor / mentor.**

3

The Changing Face of Capital Raising

Introduction

A little bit of history is provided in this chapter to show the volatility and indeed the immaturity of the system we use for raising capital. A crystal ball would be a very useful tool and it's often good to try to understand history to forecast change. In 100 years, historians will reflect on the early 21st century with a sly grin and the remark "imagine not having a global exchange" or "too bad they could not forecast the crash of ???"

A brief history

In 872AD travelers to China saw toilet paper for the first time.

In London in 1553, "The Mysterie and Comagnie of the Merchant Adventurers for the Discoverie of Regions, Dominions, Islands and Places Unknown", was designed to finance a quest for a passage to the riches of the East.

In 1602 in Amsterdam, the Dutch East India Company was the first company to issue stocks. The Dutch had designed a formal approach to allowing the public to become involved in company ownership.

Fortunes were made and lost, and there was nothing respectable or institution-like to prevent corrupt practices. Corruption had to be managed, often by brute force, by people involved in the game.

In 1698 John Casting issued a list of London stock and commodity prices at a local coffee trading house.

In 1792, 24 stock brokers signed an agreement that created the New York Stock and Exchange Board, and by 1801 the London Exchange provided the first formal system of trading which removed much but not all of the corruption.

In the 1930s the number of stock traders worldwide was very low. To be involved in the stock market you needed to be patient and wealthy. It was a cumbersome process and broker fees were high.

Many people were only now learning that it was preferable to put your money in the bank. Many still did not trust banks and many were still not understanding the concept of compound bank interest. The vast majority of the population did not trade shares.

So what's changing?

Today, it's very different with almost all involved in the share market in some way, albeit through their retirement funds. Whereas in the 1930s mothers and fathers would tell their children to save their pennies through a bank account; today our children are told of diversified portfolios.

As a result of these recent and dramatic changes, the stock market is a vibrant device. Daily share trading volumes in the past 10 years on the New York Stock Exchange have increased from 500,000 to 1,800,000 which is a remarkable increase. Much is to do with the increased involvement of individual investors, and a significant portion is provided indirectly through retirement funds. Keep in mind that this daily trading volume growth does not take into account the growth of share prices; nor does it allow for the fact that much of the returns from stocks is through dividends.

Through our short history in finance, we've seen significant new industries emerge. Analysis of hard drive manufacturers during the personal computer boom was similar to that of the railways in earlier days. Many companies failed or were taken over by the bigger players. Huge profits were made and today transport operators and hard drive manufacturers run relatively efficient plant and distribution systems.

Today, as always, volatility is normal in the stock market. No one has a crystal ball and fluctuations occur based on many elements outside those that will affect the company profits. With price to earnings (PE) ratios of over 20 for many stocks it's not difficult to understand that a ten percent stock price fall is always possible regardless of how well the company is performing.

Increased awareness of early-stage ventures by investors

Early-stage ventures are a risky investment and valuation is more difficult to determine when comparing to a listed stock.

The upside, however, is very attractive. As a simple example, an early-stage venture bought at a valuation of $1 million that lists or is sold through a trade sale with a PE ratio of 10 with $10 million in profits provides a 100 times return to the angel investor who backed the venture. An investment of $100,000 would return well over $50 million after tax and expenses. Angel investors, as we all know, are interested in helping young companies generate these kinds of returns for their investment.

What's changing is that people with the ability to invest in early-stage investments are beginning to realize that there are ways to reduce risk and to generate real returns. Angels groups are being started based on new models that consider the reduction of risk paramount. This book in itself is part of the change that is occurring. For the first time we are discussing the importance of entrepreneurs, investors and mentors operating as a single team with a single goal.

It's one of the many small changes that will shape angel investing over the next decade.

Understanding why angels don't invest in all ventures

When an investor makes their first $100,000 investment in an early-stage venture and lose their money they are not happy. Of the many outcomes, one is the loss of this investor's confidence to invest again. The investor is taken out of the market with some of the following comments:

1. I did not realize it would become a family business with no opportunity for an exit
2. They kept coming back and asking for more money
3. I worked with the entrepreneur but they did not listen
4. My spouse will kill me if I do it again
5. The venture did not succeed

Investors are often people you meet in everyday life. They may invest in many deals or may only invest in one. They like to think they know what they are talking about and they often do. In general, the experiences of a first time angel investor are limited and although they may offer some great experience to the team, they may also make mistakes as we all do.

If an investor invests the same $100,000 and wins they are very easily ready to invest again. Securing an angel investment for your venture is very much a privilege and a huge responsibility.

Growing angels groups

A number of angels groups have taken these issues and addressed them in an unusual way. Typically angels groups have formed by investors with a formal structure and a mandate to invest a minimum amount every year to maintain membership. This has worked in the past; however, many such groups fail within a few years. The model does work and certainly it enhances the early-stage investment environment.

Groups have formed, through the Angels Institute, without the mandate to invest. Members of these angels groups include mentors who are unable to invest funds directly. By not insisting on investment, groups are formed by people who want to assist early-stage ventures. Further, without the mandate to invest, the group is less likely to invest in a venture that has not yet proven that it is investor ready. This like-minded approach creates a social group with a real interest in getting together. Bringing in mentors has proven to be extremely important because these members are critical in researching, nurturing and supporting the ventures both before and after investment. Both mentors and investors "invest" time and/or money to secure an equity position in the ventures they eventually back. Mentors may also be compensated through the investment where appropriate.

This approach has proven to be appealing to those involved in the early-stage investment community. Mentors are very pleased to be rubbing shoulders with investors, knowing that their likelihood of being supported is enhanced. Investors equally value the fact that they have mentors capable of reducing some of the risk in the investment. As a team the group can improve the outcomes of their investments significantly.

An additional benefit to this structure results from the potential need for follow-on investment. Angel groups are generally limited to investments under $1 million. Many opportunities will require second level funding beyond this limit. The good news here is that as a group they have the increased attention of venture capital and private equity players. It is possible for the group to pre-arrange the second round, subject to performance, before the angels invest.

Venture capital and private equity firms can find this attractive. Not only do they receive access to quality deal-flow, but they also generate a potential investment that are better prepared and that require less maintenance by their busy investment managers.

Is investment available?

It's not now and never will be easy to raise funds for a venture. This is not because the money is not available, but because becoming investor ready is a complex and difficult process. Too many entrepreneurs believe they are investor ready when they are not. This book is intended to provide information to make this process easier for all involved. If you are truly investor ready, you will find the funds required to take your company where it needs to go.

Venture capital is more elusive than angel investment. Larger funding is available but it is difficult to secure

Start-ups seeking capital need to know that venture capital is difficult to secure.

How angels and angel groups work together

The Angels Institute has been a catalyst for a number of angels groups over the past few years and has developed a vibrant angels network.

Angels Institute has used Angelsoft as a tool to coordinate investments and to share information between investors.

Angels groups are private groups. What one group does is not generally public information. However, investments are often shared between angels and angel groups.

Below is an example of a listing from the Angels Institute private website used by angels. Such an opportunity can be shared effectively and efficiently between groups and this has become a common occurrence.

Such sharing of deals may be to increase diversification by members or to attract a particular skill set to assist the venture directly.

Summary

Angels are finding compelling reasons to invest in early-stage ventures which is good news for entrepreneurs. The process of investing in early-stage ventures is improving and assisting in reducing the risk in this volatile environment. Companies seeking capital must be investment ready if they stand any chance of securing the funds available from the early-stage investment community.

4

Understanding Equity Investment

Financing for the commercialization of ideas, particularly 'blue sky', high technology ideas, with substantial growth potential, may be obtained from angels. Angels are most often equity investors who inject capital and management skills, provide business contacts, do not charge fees and do not require a house as security.

In the 1980s a number of venture capital organizations existed but most had their fingers badly burnt in the following recession. Most small business operators and entrepreneurs realize that as a result of the trouble the banks found themselves in during the early 1990s, their tighter lending policies have made it very difficult to fund sound business ideas and expansion.

The current resurgence of angel investment remains quite logical and further activity in this area is expected to increase dramatically over time.

What is an angel?

Angels are aware that they operate in a relatively high-risk market and will usually obtain expert advice when making investment decisions.

Angels originated in New Youk where the funding of Broadway shows is common place by investors who realize they will not win every time but that many shows produce huge returns.

The original stage show of HAIR back in the late 1960s produced huge returns for its backers and investors, which are still being talked about. Interestingly a revival of this show in 2001, despite huge publicity, was cancelled months before it was due to open because of lack of advance bookings. This is a golden rule for commercializing ideas - ascertain if there is a market for the product.

Angels in general:
- Are male
- Hold a post graduate degree (typically in business, law or economics)
- Are between 31 and 65 years
- Are successful business people and experienced entrepreneurs

- Are involved in business
- Have an interest in technology and/or in the early-stage business environment

Some characteristics of angels

Angels and mainstream venture capital providers have a lot of common characteristics, however there are some key differences:

- Angels will generally look at much smaller investments (from $50,000 as a group. i.e. as low as $5,000 each).
- Angels will look at businesses in earlier stages of the business cycle.
- Angels are more likely to be "hands-on" in the early stages.
- Angels may put money directly into your business or they may provide personal guarantees for loans or leases.
- Angel groups may take many forms. Some are simply wealthy individuals syndicating for investment, and others, encourage mentors to join their groups so that more than just funds are provided to reduce the risk of the investment.
- Angel groups also tend to have a preference in investments. Some may prefer localized investment so they can keep an eye on the company and some may have a special interest like IT, marine, biotech, etc.

Pitching to investors

Pitching, sometimes referred to as the "elevator pitch", is a short and concise presentation designed to generate enough interest from an investor to enlist them in a more detailed presentation.

Business investment pitching events provide a means for investment ready (or close to investment ready) opportunities to present to public and private investment forums.

The formats for pitching varies. One group provides a strict four minute pitch by the entrepreneur followed by six minutes of question and answer.

The four minute limit is important because if forces the entrepreneur to have thought very carefully about the items most important to attract the interest of the investor. Four minutes is very restrictive and most cannot get everything they need across to the investor. The six minutes of question time is designed to get a little more across to the investors and to assist the entrepreneur. The key is to secure the attention of the investor so that additional time is available in subsequent meetings.

Finding angels

Finding angels does not assist if your venture is not yet investment ready. Becoming investment ready is the first priority and this book should partially assist in this process. If you think you are investment ready, then talk to one of the many consultants and government employees involved in the early-stage environment. See chapter 9 for access to various support avenues. They will tell you if you are ready to approach investors. Doing so before you are ready is not recommended.

Angels are an elusive group. They don't want to be approached by entrepreneurs directly but would prefer that a trusted source provide the entry point. Your lawyer and/or accountant may provide the first steps in this process.

Asked recently how long it takes to raise funds for a company, we responded with the standard three months which is very typical if the company is prepared.

We were then asked how long it would take for a venture that was truly investment ready with an awesome team, huge market and upside. We replied that if it was that good and well prepared, probably two weeks would do the job. We've seen many companies raise funds over many years and the typical three months is the rule. It's very rare to find a company that is truly investment ready.

The Angels Institute (www.angelsinstitute.com) allows entrepreneurs to enter their data for access by angels. If you take the time to apply you will need to provide the answers to a number of questions. Your company is then listed for many angels to see. While good to be exposed to angels a personal introduction is the preferred means of approaching any group. With a personal introduction, each angel will be more confident that you represent a viable opportunity.

Many of the groups listed in the tables in appendices will be able to point you in the right direction. Don't be afraid to ask for assistance. See additional tips later in this chapter on finding money.

Similar to within a good business plan, the following are considered to be the basics of a pitch:

The four minute pitch

INTRODUCTION (15 seconds), a single sentence on:

- Your name and company name
- The product or service you provide
- The uniqueness of your product/service

INDUSTRY (30 seconds)

- In what industry are you competing?
- Size, rate of growth and projected growth of the industry
- Industry trends
- Major competitors

PRODUCT/SERVICE (100 seconds)

- What is unique about your product or service?
- How or why it serves a need
- Competitive advantages
- Target customer profile
- Expected pricing and how it compares to competition
- Break even in sales/units

MANAGEMENT (30 seconds)

- Your relevant experience (but not your life history!)
- Your management team's qualifications
- Recent company history

FINANCING (30 seconds)

- How much money do you need?
- Do you want debt or equity?
- What will you use money for?
- Equipment, inventory, etc.?
- Do you have a business plan available?

CLOSE (20 seconds)

Summarize in one or two sentences. Make sure that you practice your pitch before the event. Can you use visual aids to make your pitch more successful? Be prepared for questions afterwards.

Working with an angel

Many angels, having retired early or been retrenched with a large payout, are keen to keep their hand in by offering support to growth businesses.

With both venture capitalists and angels, the equity investor acquires an agreed proportion of the company in return for the requisite funding.

Equity finance offers the significant advantage of having no interest charges. It is patient capital that seeks a return through long term capital gain rather than immediate and regular interest payments.

Equity investors have no security except for the company itself and therefore are exposed to the risk of the company failing. As a result the equity investor will look for investment opportunities in companies which have the ability to grow very successfully and produce higher returns to compensate for the risk.

When equity investors take a shareholding in a business they become part owners and typically require a seat on the company's board of directors.

They tend to take a minority share and usually do not take day-to-day control of the business, although they may be interested in attending regular management meetings and review monthly accounts. The equity investor usually acts as a mentor and aims to provide support and advice on a range of management and technical issues to assist the company to develop its full potential.

According to R.J. Gaston, a U.S. based angel, potential investors can be classified thus:

- **Business devils:** Investors who obtain absolute majority control (51 percent or more of voting equity).
- **Godfathers:** Successful, often semi-retired business people who want to act as mentors to stay active in the business world.
- **Peers**: Business owners who invest in family businesses only.
- **Uncle angels:** Angels who invest in family businesses only.
- **Income-based angels:** Investors from professions such as medicine, law and accounting.
- **Executive angels:** Business executives with some success in large corporations who want to run an entire business.
- **Super rich investors.**
- **High-tech angels:** Investors interested only in investing in firms that manufacture high-technology products.
- **Silent partners:** Passive shareholders who seek no active role in the firm.
- **Opportunists:** Investors who seek large investment shares for small outlays.

Requirements and expectations of angels

Angels have preferences for particular stages of investment, amount of investment, industry sectors, and geographical location.

It is important that your team have an understanding of the requirements of angels and their expectations before approaching them with your proposal. A good analogy is that any good salesperson will take time to understand their prospective client and learn what expectations they have before making an approach. As we mention elsewhere in this book, you will only get one chance to make a first impression.

- **Superior businesses**. Angels look for companies with superior products or services. For leveraged management buyouts - companies with high borrowing capacity, stability of earnings and an ability to generate surplus cash to quickly repay debt.
- **Quality and depth of management**. The firm needs quality and depth in the management team.
- **Corporate governance and structure.** The investee company has to be willing to adopt modern corporate governance standards. A proprietary limited company is an almost mandatory requirement.
- **Ownership**. Clear ownership of the business structure and assets by the operating company. An appropriate investment structure. An attractive business opportunity. To structure a satisfactory deal to produce the anticipated financial returns to investors.
- **An exit plan**. Angels look for clear exit routes for their investment such as an NASDAQ, NYSE or AMEX public listing or a third party acquisition of the investee company.

Potential investors will expect your team:
- To be able to clearly explain the advantages of them investing in your business.
- To be able to backup your claims and promises with up-to-date accounts and information.
- To 'sell' your ideas, concepts and strategies to them in a convincing manner.
- To understand and appreciate the degree of risk as they perceive it.
- To have a clear and concise business plan which will work and which is capable of being implemented.
- To have the ability to work with them.
- In the majority of cases the potential investors are more interested in investing in the person rather than the idea or concept.
- To have the ability to exit the investment through the company listing on the stock exchange, selling to a trade buyer or through a management buyout.

The initial meeting - screening by the angel

The initial meeting provides an opportunity:
- For the investor to meet with the venture team.
- To meet with key members of the venture team.
- To review the business plan.
- To conduct initial due diligence on the project.
- Make sure that your team arrives on time and dresses to impress - look and present as someone who means business. You will never get another chance to make a first impression!

The initial meeting is an important time for the venture team - maximize the opportunity.
- Be thoroughly prepared - your team should have rehearsed your presentation and have a professional business plan which indicates that you are investment ready.
- Your team should be able to present some visual aids to reinforce your proposal. A sample or prototype of your product is a must. Make sure that it

is defect free and works as it should. A laptop computer can provide the opportunity to demonstrate your concept using a PowerPoint presentation.
- Use this meeting as an opportunity for your team to demonstrate their understanding of their business.
- It is an opportunity for your team to demonstrate their ability to achieve the strategies outlined in the business plan and their ability to bring the project to profitable commercialization.
- The angels will use this meeting to look carefully at the team's functional skills and backgrounds.

Steps involved in preparing for equity investment

In order to sell your business to potential investors you will need:
- To have clearly identified the direction your venture intends taking with an up to date, practical and workable business plan.
- To have identified the strengths, weaknesses, opportunities and threats facing your venture (see SWOT analysis in Chapter 2).
- To have identified the trends in your market place and industry.
- To have identified a strategy for growth and expansion.
- To have an up-to-date set of accounts.
- To be able to articulate your growth aspirations and vision with clarity, enthusiasm and passion.
- To have the ability to sell yourself and your management skills to potential investors before you sell your business ideas.
- To be able to demonstrate your venture's capital requirements, and how you will be able to service that debt.
- To have an understanding of the business environment your venture operates in and factors that may affect your market place now and in the future.
- To have an audit trail - potential investors will want to carry out due diligence on your business.
- To have your team prepared to listen to other people and heed their advice.
- To understand your legal requirement in accepting investment.

Exit strategies

Any potential investor in your venture will want a clear picture - and a written agreement - on how they will be able to sell out of the venture and recover their investment. What are some ways in which the potential investor will want to be able to exit the venture? Their expectations and exit strategies when quitting or selling out of your business would probably include:

- Selling their investment, in the later development stages, to another investor
- Selling their investment to take advantage of improved profits
- Selling their investment to pursue other opportunities
- Selling their investment back to the owner(s)
- Selling their investment and/or the business to another organization as a take-over target
- Selling the business to the company management in a Management Buyout
- Floating the company on the NSX, SIM or ASX stock exchanges via an Initial Public Offering (IPO)

Angels and commercializing your ideas

People starting their own innovative ventures are often surprised that finance is extremely difficult to secure in order to bring their idea to commercialization. Many small and medium-size ventures commence with less than $10,000. Most need between $20,000 and $200,000 to initiate their venture. Many regret starting with too little money, which hampers growth plans.

Meaningful statistics on angel investment is difficult to come by. No one really knows how many innovative venture start-ups have been financed by family members. Arrangements are generally informal and are not well documented.

People need to be careful when investing in a relative's business. People have different expectations and it can become a great source of friction between family members and friends.

Typically, angels take anywhere between 15 and 50 percent of the equity in a business. If you believe your idea will work, do you want to give away 50 percent of the business? Some venture teams have a problem with this and fail to grasp that 50 percent of something tangible is worth far more than 100 percent of nothing. At a start-up stage, angels are taking a huge risk, so they ask for a lot.

Angels may want a say in how the business is run, so your venture will be effectively bringing in a partner. As anybody experienced in business realizes, in partnerships, there is often a difference of opinion, which can lead to departures.

Passing control to others can provide huge advantage and assist in generating the success of a venture. It is difficult to come to this conclusion when it is the entrepreneur's baby, however, in the hands of experienced angels, successes can be improved significantly in both size and timing.

Many owners of business start-ups have no other option other than to pass on control. Banks reject most requests for start-up finance. Most of the market lends on a secured basis. The reason most start-ups are rejected is because start-ups cannot provide a track record (for example, three years of revenue and profit). If a start-up business can use a home as security, they can usually access a loan with competitive fees and conditions attached.

Many entrepreneurs complain that banks are incapable of evaluating business start-up proposals. As a result, some use expensive credit cards to finance their ventures. That approach only works for companies with very low start-up costs.

People often fail because they do not understand the costs of starting a business venture. They also do not expect the cash cycle with tax bills every quarter. The worst thing a start-up can do is use a credit card or even a bank loan without fully understanding how the cash comes in and out of a business.

Many people starting a new business approach angel groups and venture capitalists for money. Few realize that angel groups and venture capitalists increasingly specialize in funding specific parts of the growth cycle. Some focus on medium-size companies preparing to float. Others are interested only in cutting-edge technology businesses for instance.

Others provide seed funding once the business has a prototype product developed. However, like banks, many venture capital firms are unwilling to invest in a venture starting from scratch.

Tips on how to appeal to angel investors

- **Provide "proof of concept"**. Accept the fact that having "a good idea" is often not enough to raise capital from private investors, and your team should do their homework to provide "proof of concept" for your venture.
- Understand that raising capital requires an expenditure of capital.
- Identify and contact angels or angel groups who are suitable for you.
- Recognize that industry experience is valuable and important to angel investors. A business is more likely to succeed if you at least have one or two parties experienced in the industry area you are pursuing, so that the skills of the angel investor become an "adjunct" to your team.
- Recognize that raising capital takes time. It is not unusual for a start-up entrepreneurial team to spend 50-70 percent of their time raising capital from angel investors, a process that can last on average for three to six months.
- During that time, angel investors will ask numerous detailed questions as part of their due diligence process and will raise objections in regard to your market, marketing strategy, technology, operations, or competitive landscape.
- Recognize that angels are "value-added investors."
- Never stop looking for additional angel investors until all checks from interested parties have cleared the bank. Relying on expectations or promises alone can place a venture in jeopardy.
- Generate confidence in your angel by investing your own money in your venture.
- Develop investor credibility by securing funding from various government programs.

Are you investor ready?

Can you concisely and efficiently present your pitch to investors?
- Have you assessed your capital requirements?
- Can you explain the reasons you wish to raise extra capital?
- Can you prove you have a fantastic team dedicated to generating success?
- Do you have up-to-date accounts on hand?
- Do you have a workable business plan in place?

- Can you communicate your business directions and vision verbally and concisely?
- Are you comfortable working with people who may be smarter than you and who may be better educated than you?
- Does your business have a mission statement?
- Have you analyzed past performance?
- How do you compare against an industry profile?
- Have you identified critical factors for success?
- Have you decided on profit targets?
- Have you set efficiency standards?
- Have you planned several years ahead in summary?
- Have you detailed next year's plan by month?
- Have you checked sales projections?
- Have you projected financial resources?
- Have you prepared a weekly cash flow?
- Have you a plan for exit?

Most angels see themselves as value-added investors, meaning that they derive as much personal satisfaction from helping a new business owner as they do from contributing capital to the venture. Many were previously successful business owners.

Angels bring with them "value added" benefits including: prior industry experience, valuable knowledge about business itself, their ability to mentor, creative ideas, contacts for your business.

Entrepreneurs who expect investors to risk their money in their venture, should also place at least 20 percent of their own net worth in their business. Those entrepreneurs who are not willing to assume such risk are not considered serious entrepreneurs by the investment community, and will most likely not receive any funding.

What are the difficulties of working on your own as an angel?

The first problem area is one of finding quality deal-flow. Wealthy angels are sought after and have developed a network to both filter deal-flow to those suiting his/her interests and reducing the number of opportunities looked at. Newer investors will often see the deals that others have turned away. If you rush into investing in these you will probably be an angel of short life expectancy. Joining a group of other like-minded individuals serves to provide protection and assist in exposure to worthwhile deal-flow.

The next problem is actually doing a deal once you have found an opportunity. Do you have the specialist knowledge required to carry out due diligence, structure the investment giving due thought to your planned exit and write up shareholders'

Angel Investors look for innovative ventures and companies with superior products or services targeted at fast growing or untapped markets with a defensible strategic position.

A strong or potentially strong export potential is also important.

... they are seeking companies with high borrowing capacity, stability of earnings and an ability to generate surplus cash to quickly repay debt.

agreements and articles? The answer is probably no, in which case you will need an accountant and a lawyer and maybe an industry expert for the industrial due diligence side of things.

On your own this can cost a disproportionate amount of the invested sum and bear in mind you will probably have a few false starts – in short, you might have spent quite a large sum of money before you actually get to complete a transaction.

Once you have completed an investment your next difficulties are managing the investment and finding a suitable exit. Common scenarios are; firstly you have a falling out with the board, secondly the main shareholders decide to run the company as a lifestyle business and thirdly, the company needs a second and third round of funding – is your pocket deep enough and are you going to follow your money in what might be a distress refinancing?

Recent history shows that angels who operate in groups are generally more successful - hence the evolution of the Founders Forum, the Angels Institute and the resulting growth of angels groups.

The pros and cons of angel investment

The benefits and advantages of using an Angel

- The provision of long term equity finance to provide a solid capital base for future growth.
- Enabling your business to grow and expand and enter new markets quicker than it could otherwise
- Sharing both the risks and rewards
- Practical advice and assistance to the company based on past experience
- A network of contacts
- The angel may be capable of providing additional rounds of funding
- Their primary return on investment comes from capital gain when they eventually sell their shares in the company
- Angels are in the business of promoting growth in the companies they invest in and managing the associated risk to protect and enhance their investors' capital.

- When an investor puts money into your business some changes are inevitable:
- The investor will probably insist upon monthly financial reports, which may be checked by an independent third party
- The investor will probably insist upon regular meetings to update progress
- Control of the business will probably be shared
- The owner loses their complete autonomy
- Commercial secrets will be shared
- Finances will be under constant scrutiny
- The investor may want to have a say in day-to-day operations
- The investor may want you to take more or less business risks
- Other associates of the investor may want to have access to you
- There may be changes which you perceive as negative and which may generate friction.

Some possible disadvantages of using an Angel

Understanding equity investment

Equity investment is a means of financing innovative ventures and fast growing private companies. Finance may be required for the start-up, development/expansion or purchase of a company via a mechanism such as in a management buyout.

Growing businesses always require capital. There are a number of alternative methods to fund growth. These include the owner's own capital, arranging debt finance, or seeking an equity partner, as is the case with angel investment.

All businesses have a 'life cycle' which involves a number of stages of growth and development. Investors refer to these stages when making investments. Briefly, they are as follows:

Pre-Seed/Seed. The company is at the idea stage or may be in the process of being organized and needs finance for research and development. This is often funded by the entrepreneur's own resources.

Start-up/early-stage. The company is in the process of being set up or may have been in business for a short time. The company may have "proof of concept", may not have sold their product commercially and has little or no track record. Investee companies have completed the product development stage and require funds to initiate commercial manufacturing and sales.

Early Expansion The company is now established and requires capital for further growth and expansion. The company may or may not have made a profit at this stage but has obtained "proof of sales". This is a period of rapid growth and the company will usually require several rounds of capital injection as it achieves the milestones set in the business plan.

Venture capital and private equity

Management Buyout (MBO) These are funds provided to enable a current operating management and investors to acquire an existing product or business from a public or private company.

Management Buy-In (MBI) These are funds provided to enable a manager or group of managers from outside the company to buy in to the company. The size of investment is closely related to the stage of investment.

On the whole, early-stage investments require less capital than an expansion or MBO stage. Equity investors spend the same amount of time and effort assessing and assisting an early-stage company as they do a later-stage company. In fact, the earlier stage companies usually require greater assistance than later-stage companies.

Therefore, many equity capital firms prefer to invest in later-stage lower risk deals that fit their investment criteria.

Typical Small and Medium Enterprises (SME's) are businesses which have between one and 250 employees. SME's currently generate 45 percent of the GDP and employ at least 50 percent of the work force. Growth in this business sector should have a significant impact on overall economic growth, export performance and employment.

Venture capital firms have funds specializing in particular industry sectors such as bioscience, information, technology or manufacturing. Many firms will actively avoid investing in sectors such as property, mining and farming.

Venture capitalists tend to have investments within a reasonable proximity of their central and regional offices.

There are a number of advantages of venture capital over other forms of finance, such as:

- It provides long term equity finance which provides a solid capital base for future growth.
- The venture capitalist is a business partner, sharing both the risks and rewards. Venture capitalists are rewarded by business success and the capital gain.
- The venture capitalist is able to provide practical advice and assistance to the company based on past experience with other companies which were in similar situations.
- The venture capitalist usually has a network of contacts in many areas that can add value to the company, such as in recruiting key personnel, providing contacts in international markets, introductions to strategic partners, and if needed co-investments with other venture capital firms when additional rounds of financing are required.
- The venture capitalist may be capable of providing additional rounds of funding should it be required to finance growth.

Venture capital firms typically source the majority of their funding from large investment institutions such as retirement funds and banks.

These institutions invest in a venture capital fund for a period of up to 10 years, and have expectations of higher than average returns on the investment. The venture capital firm acts as a fund manager, identifying and investigating investment opportunities, managing the investment process and exiting the investment to realize profits.

To compensate for the long term commitment and lack of both security and liquidity, investment institutions expect to receive very high returns on their investment.

Venture capitalists typically exit the investment through the company listing on the stock exchange, selling to a trade buyer or through a management buyout.

Although the venture capitalist may receive some return through dividends, their primary return on investment comes from capital gain when they eventually sell their shares in the company, typically between three to seven years after the investment.

Venture capitalists are therefore in the business of promoting growth in the companies they invest in and managing the associated risk to protect and enhance their investors' capital.

A venture capitalist typically seeks:

Superior businesses

Venture capitalists look for innovative ventures and companies with superior products or services targeted at fast growing or untapped markets with a defensible strategic position. A strong or potentially strong export potential is also important.

Alternatively for leveraged management buyouts, they are seeking companies with high borrowing capacity, stability of earnings and an ability to generate surplus cash to quickly repay debt.

Quality and depth of management

Venture capitalists must be confident that the innovative venture has the quality and depth in the management team to achieve its aspirations. Venture capitalists seldom seek managerial control, rather they want to add value to the investment where they have particular skills including fund raising, mergers and acquisitions, international marketing and networks.

Realistic business valuation

A key ingredient in any successful negotiation for funding is a realistic business valuation. Invariably the business owner will place a much higher valuation on the business than the Venture Capitalist because of the perceived future potential.

Unfortunately it is often difficult to put a concise value on this "blue sky". The valuation of intellectual property is also difficult, especially without proven sales results. The more developed a business is the higher the valuation will be.

A company seeking seed or start-up capital will have a much lower valuation than the same business once it has product and sales. Business owners will often "bootstrap" business development, tapping all possible sources of finance before seeking venture capital to maximize the value of their company.

Selecting a venture capitalist

Prior to selecting a venture capitalist, the entrepreneur should study the particular investment preferences set down by the venture capital firm. Often venture capitalists have preferences for particular stages of investment, amount of investment, industry sectors, and geographical location.

Once a short-list of potential venture capitalists has been drawn up, it is often a good idea to contact the venture capital firm and request a copy of their own publications which will further clarify the type of investments they favor.

An investment in an unlisted company has a long term horizon, typically four to six years. It is important to select venture capitalists with whom it is possible to have a good working relationship.

Often businesses do not meet their cash flow forecasts and require additional funds, so an investor's ability to invest further funds if required is also important.

Finally, when choosing a venture capitalist, the entrepreneur should consider not just the amount and terms of investments, but also the additional value that the venture capitalist can bring to the company.

These skills may include industry knowledge, fund raising, financial and strategic planning, recruitment of key personnel, mergers and acquisitions, and access to international markets and technology.

Venture capitalists are higher risk investors and, in accepting these higher risks, they desire a higher return on their investment. The risk/reward ratio is managed by the venture capitalist by only investing in businesses which fit their investment criteria.

No two venture capitalists are identical with each having a slightly different operating approach. The differences may relate to location of the business, the size of the investment, the stage of the company, industry specialization, structure of the investment and involvement of the venture capitalists in the company's activities.

The entrepreneur should not be discouraged if one venture capitalist does not wish to proceed with an investment in the company; an important part of the entrepreneurial mindset is the ability to handle rejection and adversity!

The rejection may not be a reflection of the quality of the business, but rather a matter of the business not fitting with the venture capitalists particular investment criteria.

The investment process

The investment process begins with the venture capitalist conducting an initial review of the proposal to determine if it fits with the firm's investment criteria. If so, a meeting will be arranged with the entrepreneur/management team to discuss the business plan.

Preliminary screening

The initial meeting provides an opportunity for the venture capitalist to meet with the entrepreneur and key members of the management team to review the business plan and conduct initial due diligence on the project. It is an important time for the management team to demonstrate their understanding of their business and ability to achieve the strategies outlined in the plan. The venture capitalist will look carefully at the team's functional skills and backgrounds.

Negotiating investment

This involves an agreement between the venture capitalist and management of the terms of a memorandum of understanding (or a term sheet). The venture capitalist will then proceed to study the viability of the market to estimate its potential. Often they use market forecasts which have been independently prepared by industry experts who specialize in estimating the size and growth rates of markets and market segments. The venture capitalist also studies the industry carefully to obtain information about competitors, entry barriers, the potential to exploit substantial niches, product life cycles, distribution channels and possible export potential. The due diligence continues with reports from accountants and other consultants.

Due diligence and negotiating investment

Approvals and investment completed

The process involves exhaustive due diligence and disclosure of all relevant business information. Final terms can then be negotiated and an investment proposal submitted to the board of directors. If approved, legal documents are prepared.

A shareholders' agreement is prepared containing the rights and obligations of each party. This could include, for example, veto rights by the investor on remuneration and loans to executives, acquisition or sale of assets, audit, listing of the company, rights of co-sale and warranties relating to the accuracy of information enclosed.

After the preliminary investigation, the venture capitalist and management will agree on the terms of a Memorandum of Understanding outlining the intentions of both parties. The venture capitalist will then commence the due diligence process including:

- A comprehensive market analysis including independent market research, market segmentation and growth potential

- Specific industry analysis
- Competitors analysis
- Analysis of barriers to entry
- Analysis of the potential to exploit substantial niches
- Product life cycle
- Distribution channels and possible export potential
- Accounting and legal due diligence

The investment process can take up to three months, and sometimes longer. It is important therefore not to expect a speedy response. It is advisable to plan the business financial needs early on to allow appropriate time to secure the required funding.

Shareholders' agreement

It is likely that a shareholders' agreement would be prepared containing the rights and obligations of each party. This could include:
- Amount and terms of investment
- Dividend policy
- Composition of the board of directors
- Reporting - management reports, monthly accounts, annual budgets
- Liquidity (exit) plans
- Rights of co-sale
- Warranties
- Matters requiring venture capitalist approval (such as auditors, employment contracts, major asset purchases, major debt obligations and significant variations of plans)

The objective of these agreements is to clarify the relationship and protect the interest of each party in the business. When most small and medium business operators wish to expand they usually have to look for debt finance from a typically apathetic bank manager, or remortgage their homes. See Chapter 17 for further detail on shareholders'

Angels - equity investment

The current flat property market and volatile share market are some factors which make investing in innovative business opportunities attractive to angels.

Angels complain that the biggest problem they face is dealing with business proprietors and venture teams who are not 'investment ready' – "they cannot communicate or think clearly or laterally".

A further complaint is that it takes from three to six months for these business proprietors and venture teams to become 'investment ready'. And they are usually bent in one direction and obsessed with their project.

An angel will expect your venture team to be able to explain clearly and succinctly what your project is about - your vision, goals and commitment. People who are paranoid about secrecy or unable to clearly articulate what their business is about will usually receive a poor hearing from angels.

Further, an angel will also expect you to be able to explain clearly and succinctly, backed up with cash flow statements and projections, how much money you need straight away and how much more money you will require over the term of the project.

When your venture takes on an investor, that investor - it may be a person or company - will have a number of expectations in regard to your team and your business.

Most investors would expect your team to have a proprietary limited (Pty Ltd) company with a certain number of paid up shares and an agreed amount of issued capital, so that they can be issued shares in return for, and as tangible proof of their investment.

Most importantly, your investor or angel will expect a return on their investment.

If you are unable to pay regular interest or dividends to your angel and they have to wait years for a return on their investment, then it follows that they will have expectations of a high return - perhaps in the order of 40-50 percent or more.

It is not unusual for angels to be putting up more cash than the business owner. Typically the business owner will be contributing the "perspiration" and intellectual property such as patents on new products or technology, while the angel provides the working capital.

Would you like someone to invest in your venture?

Many business proprietors and venture teams would welcome extra working capital, and indeed many would also welcome the input and new objectivity that an investor could (and should) bring to their business.

In reality however, very few business proprietors and venture teams are at a stage where they are ready to meet the expectations of investors or angels, and they are usually unable to communicate effectively with potential investors.

The advantages and disadvantages of equity investment

Equity investment should enable your innovative venture to grow and expand and enter new markets quicker than it could otherwise. The sustainable competitive advantage of your venture should be improved. Existing profitability should be at least maintained and ideally, exponentially improved.

Equity investment will usually allow your venture to use the working capital provided without having to make periodic interest repayments - the angel is prepared to wait for a return on their investment. An extra injection of capital should increase the barriers to entry to that market by competitors.

An investor should provide you and your business with a new objectivity and an extra base of experience to draw upon. Further, an investor should provide you with access to new networks.

After investment, changes are inevitable:

- The investor will probably insist upon monthly financial reports, which may be checked by an independent third party
- The investor will probably insist upon regular meetings to update progress
- Control of the business will probably be shared
- The owner loses their complete autonomy
- Commercial secrets will be shared
- Finances will be under constant scrutiny
- The investor may want to have a say in day-to-day operations
- The investor may want you to take more or less business risks
- Other associates of the investor may want to have access to you

- Inevitably there will be positive changes - e.g. more input into decision making, resulting in better decisions
- There may also be changes which you perceive as negative and which may generate friction

Ownership versus control

One of the regular sticking points in negotiations with equity investors is the issue of respective shareholdings.

The investor will be seeking a significant equity position, without removing the much needed motivation of the founders, for the minimum investment. The venture team will want to raise as much capital as possible while giving away minimum equity. This conflicting situation must be resolved through negotiation, the outcome must be fair and equitable to both parties for a successful business relationship.

Business owners often place too much emphasis on maintaining at least 51 percent shareholding in the company because of the fear of losing control of the business. When dealing with venture capitalists and angels it should be remembered that they do not want to run your business on a day-to-day basis. Their profit and return is dependent on the success of you and your business and they will assist you as far as possible to succeed.

When seeking an equity investor a business owner should consider the long-term situation. The vision should be one of wealth generation and maximum return on investment for all shareholders. To illustrate this, a growing company may undertake several rounds of capital raising, starting with original shareholders through to angels, venture capital and possible public listing. At each subsequent stage the founder's shareholding decreases and is diluted, but the value of the founder's equity increases.

Dilution or agreements with shareholders will often remove control from the founder. As a team, you, company mentors and investors want the same thing, a successful company. If you are not the person to drive the ship, you need to understand that it makes sense to remove you, and it's in your best interest to do so. If you are the right person then it will be unanimous to keep you in that position. If you are the only one who thinks you are the right person, it's time to listen to the investors very carefully. They don't seek to battle, they seek the best solution for the shareholders.

If you do find yourself in such a position where you are unhappy with the potential of being removed as the company leader, keep in mind that you can seek a white knight, willing to take out the other investors and leave you in charge.

The old adage about having a small percentage of a million dollar company rather than 100 percent of nothing certainly rings true.

Raising capital

In a recent newspaper interview, the managing director of an investment banking organization with special interests in servicing the family business sector, made the following points:

- All businesses need to raise capital to allow proper growth and expansion.
- There can be specific problems when there is no clear differentiation between the family and the business.
- They need to get themselves investment ready.
- The process is to have a proper set of accounts and proper corporate governance in place - that is separate personal, business and formal board meetings.

- The business plan needs to be an active program for business, now, and for the future.
- They need to think about whether they will retain earnings, get more money from the family, or borrow from a bank.
- The business will need to have all these things in place, otherwise no outside person will put money into the company and if the business is going to get money from the family or internally, there can be problems if things are not structured properly.
- ... it is important to have the formal structures in place and set out a plan of what needs to be done to promote growth.
- The business needs to live up to the business plan.
- Use up all the available capital from family and friends, then borrow from a bank, and after that go outside for capital ... an angel.
- The main thing is if the business is going to be successful in the long run, then the most expensive price you pay for capital is equity.
- Where a business is paying in equity it is better to raise it later than sooner. Then you can raise more money by selling less of the company when you are more successful, using the price earnings ratio.
- Many people have not separated family interests from the business. Families must look on the business as an investment, not as an employer for family members.

"The loss was a result of an egomaniac that refused to compromise or even recognize possible limitations to the market opportunity or to his talent!"

Angel describing one failed deal

Equity investment - The advantages and disadvantages

Advantages
- Less exposure to interest rates
- More stable financial structure
- Raise funds in excess of security
- Equity investment should enable your innovative venture to grow and expand and enter new markets quicker than it could otherwise
- The sustainable competitive advantage of your venture should be improved
- Existing profitability should be at least maintained and ideally, exponentially improved
- Equity investment may allow your venture to use the working capital provided without having to make periodic interest repayments - the Angel is prepared to wait for a return on their investment
- An extra injection of capital should increase the barriers to entry to that market by competitors
- An investor should provide the venture with a new objectivity and an extra base of experience to draw upon
- An investor should provide the venture with access to new networks
- Inevitably there will be positive changes - e.g. more input into decision making, resulting in better decisions
- Any disadvantages may be balanced by the skills, knowledge and input of the investor resulting in synergy for the business

Disadvantages
- Need to identify exit within defined timeframe
- Not suitable for urgent or unplanned funding
- Control of the business will probably be shared
- The owner looses their complete autonomy
- Commercial secrets will be shared
- Finances will be under constant scrutiny
- The investor may want to have a say in day-to-day operations
- The investor may want you take more or less business risks
- Other associates of the investor may want to have access to the venture team
- There may also be changes which your team perceive as negative and which may generate friction
- The investor may insist on regular meetings to update progress

Sources of capital

Growing innovative ventures always require additional working capital. There are a number of alternative methods to raise this finance to fund growth and expansion. These methods include using the venture team's own capital, arranging debt finance, or seeking equity investment, where a third party buys shares in the business, thereby injecting cash.

Equity investment is a means of financing fast growing private companies. This type of finance may be appropriate for companies at the start-up, development and expansion stages or for specific situations such as a management buyout. Finance for your commercializing an innovative venture or assistance with finance, may potentially be obtained from a number of traditional and other institutions and sources including:

Angels. Angels can provide investment money for under-capitalized innovative ventures with little security. More details and descriptions of angels and how they can assist developing businesses are detailed in this book.

Bank loans. The bank usually requires security over property as a key requirement. Interest rates fluctuate with market conditions. Many innovative ventures and small businesses cannot access bank loans due to lack of security and lack of a strong trading history.

Bank overdrafts. Again the bank usually requires security over property as a key requirement or for your venture team to deposit money in a separate account as cover and security, usually at a higher rate than a loan, and also subject to market fluctuations. Often subject to the bank managers discretion and may be called in at short notice.

Barter. Barter transaction organizations appear to have had a number of tries at offering a serious alternative to paying money for goods or services. For an up-front fee a business is entitled to barter their goods or services with other barter organizations. Probably of little use for innovative ventures and organizations seeking capital to develop and grow.

Consignment stock. Many businesses obtain consignment stock as a method of lessening the amount of working capital required. This method has limitations, as only certain narrow product ranges may be available, and it relies on the discretion of those providing the stock.

Contra deals. Instead of paying for goods or services with money it may be possible to do contra deals with suppliers.

Credit cards. Many innovative venture teams have used one or more credit cards to finance their business. Interest rates are high and it is unusual for more than $25,000 to be available on any one card.

Factoring. Factoring is suitable for innovative ventures; it involves selling your invoices to a factoring company at a discount and receiving payment for around 80 percent of the invoice value, usually within a few days. The annualized interest rate is high. Unsuitable for many businesses as fairly high levels of turnover are usually a requirement. Some factoring companies require property as security.

Family loans. A great number of innovative ventures and businesses source unsecured finance from family members, with all the advantages and disadvantages of nepotism.

Franchising. When a business achieves a critical level of turnover and profitability it may be suitable for franchising. Obviously unsuitable for emerging and developing companies with no proven track record.

Government grants. The federal government provides a suite of programs that aim to address many of the capital, knowledge and collaborative challenges faced by entrepreneurs and start-up companies. AusIndustry are a good initial contact point; further details and information regarding Federal Government programs are provided in a later chapter of this book.

Innovation investment funds. A federal government initiative that began in 1998 and encourages investment into early-stage companies through the provision of capital to venture capital fund managers.

Joint ventures. Funding, usually for one particular project is sought from others who may be able to contribute skills as well as money. It has the advantage of minimizing losses if the project fails. Joint ventures are becoming increasingly more common in the equity marketplace, particularly for early-stage innovative ventures trying to launch new products or technology. A typical joint venture is where an established company, usually with a mature product in the market, established distribution channels, well established business infrastructure and possibly excess manufacturing capacity, will absorb the fledgling business. This is not done on a "predatory" basis, rather on a co-operative basis for the benefit of both companies.

This type of joint venture arrangement is more prevalent where there is either strong product synergy or products of a complementary nature. The key advantage to the emerging business is the reduction in the capital requirement to set up the business infrastructure and the many other associated start up costs.

The established businesses will have administration, accounting, payroll and office facilities. There will usually be manufacturing and warehousing facilities in place as well. The new business will have a running start at marketing the new product as they will be able to piggyback the name and reputation of the established business.

The advantages to the established business are also significant. Many companies find this process a cost efficient method of product diversification, effectively "outsourcing" their R&D. By taking on the young company they may also acquire a potential market competitor, thereby avoiding market fragmentation.

The structure of these joint venture arrangements can be quite flexible. For instance:

- Forming a new jointly owned "subsidiary" company.
- The new product may become an operating division.
- The new venture may be absorbed into the established business.
- Usually a management role for incoming shareholders is provided.
- There will be sharing of intellectual property (often both ways).
- The 'deal' is usually facilitated through a share swap.

These 'deals' become quite attractive because of the significant savings in cash outlay. The emerging business may contribute intellectual property and any assets in return for shares while the established business will undertake to contribute company resources (cash, labor, technical resources, manufacturing capacity, distribution channels etc.) to ensure the commercial success of the new product. These outcomes usually result in accelerated product launch and market penetration.

Leasing. Can be, and may be, an attractive option for funding the purchase of capital equipment for innovative ventures.

Management buyout (MBO). Existing companies (public or private), divisions or products, are purchased by the management and perhaps the people working there, usually with borrowed funds. Additional investors may be involved. The funds required typically exceed $1 million, and may be funded by angels, venture capital (MBO specialists), or banks/secured debt facilities.

Partners - shareholders. Developing innovative ventures and organizations can consider taking on equity partners or shareholders, for which many advantages may exist. For instance, the partner or shareholder may provide capital as well as expertise and industry contacts.

Public listing - Stock exchange float. Probably the ultimate way of raising large amounts of money to fund an innovative venture business. Very high costs are involved and of course companies usually need to have a demonstrated track record in order to secure a listing. When a company first lists on the stock exchange it is often referred to as an Initial Public Offering (IPO) . Funds raised are generally over $10 million for a listing.

Solicitors. A number of solicitors are asked by clients to invest their money in worthwhile schemes. These funds are often at higher rates of interest.

Trading terms from suppliers (creditors). A great many businesses use their unwitting and unwilling suppliers to assist in financing their own business. Instead of paying the supplier on a 30 day basis, payment is stretched to 60 or even 90 days, in many cases creating a significant amount of extra working capital.

Trading terms from customers (debtors). As a result of the recession in the early 1990s many businesses tightened up their terms to their customers and asked (and in many cases insisted) that they pay in seven days instead of 30 days. In many industries however, unless you have a unique product or service, the customer determines and sets the payment terms.

Venture capital. Money is sought from people or organizations willing to invest their money in a new idea or business venture. In the USA venture capital companies abound and have had some significant and huge wins and returns when fledgling innovative venture companies list on the stock exchange. Venture capital companies usually source funds from banks, retirement funds, insurance companies or large investment houses and use these funds to invest in a range of emerging growth businesses. In Australia the venture capital industry is relatively small but growing and is becoming an increasingly important source of business capital.

> **Typically, businesses that have the best chance of raising capital will be either "Investor Ready" or "Investment Ready"**

Accessing debt and equity finance

As you will gather it is a dynamic market place to find this type of enterprise, we suggest you consult the internet, your yellow pages or similar directory

Once a non-listed innovative venture business has found one or more potential investors they may no longer be exempt from the need to issue a prospectus. For example, you may not make an offer of securities to more than 20 parties in a 12 month period without a prospectus unless you can claim the benefit of some other prospectus exemption recognized under the Law.

Entrepreneurial evaluation, Harvard style

The Harvard Framework for investment opportunities was developed at the Harvard Business School by William Sahlman and Howard Stevenson[4].

Sahlman and Stevenson assert that, rather than judge entrepreneurs or their business plans as winners or losers, it is most productive to look at the investment opportunity as an interconnected combination of four elements: people, context, business opportunity, and deal. The right combination, which is often manageable, means a high-potential opportunity. A bad combination, or the lack of any single element, is a recipe for failure. Most important, within any investment opportunity, there is usually some potential for a win, if only the right investor would join it, or if the right changes would be made. If you integrate this philosophy of investing into your thinking, according to Sahlman and Stevenson, you will be a far better investor.

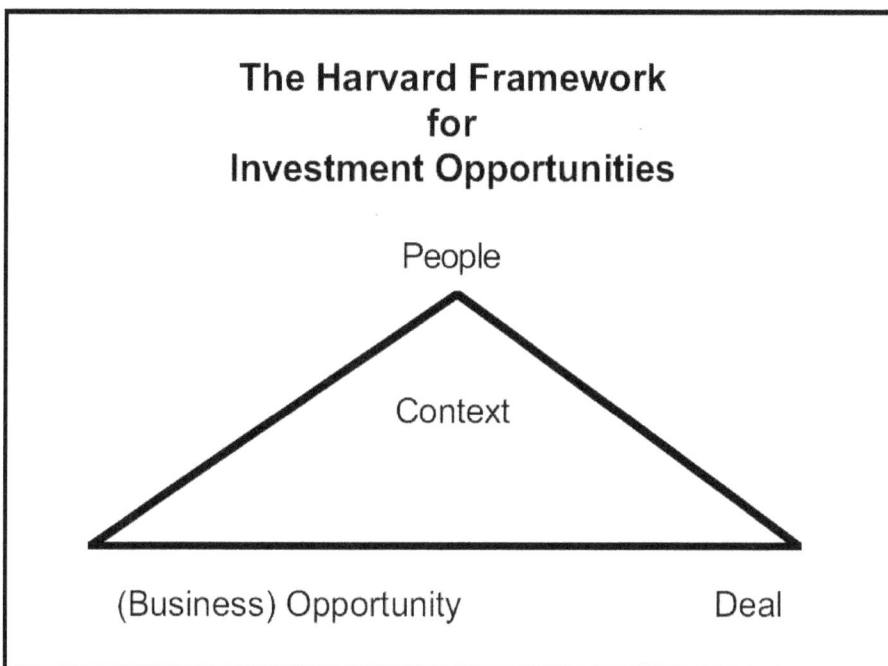

The Harvard Framework for Investment Opportunities

People

Context

(Business) Opportunity   Deal

The elements:

People. The people in the deal, including the entrepreneur, team members, investors, advisors, and any significant stakeholders.

Business opportunity. The potential business opportunity, which includes the business model, the size (which implies the potential returns), the customers, and the window within which it can be seized.

Context. The macro-situation, which includes external factors, such as: technology development, customer desires, the state of the economy, industry trends, etc.

Deal. The structure of the deal, its terms and pricing.

---

[4] Harvard Business School, Sept 24, 2001 David Amis and Howard Stevenston (referencing Winning Angels: the 7 Fundamentals of Early-Stage Investing, Pearson Education Limited, 2001)

Not only is each element critical by itself, but the way they interact is also crucial. For example, in one opportunity at a US venture capital organization, a web developer with $5 million in sales was raising its first round of capital on a $10 million valuation.

Two comparable companies in the marketplace were worth over $1 billion each, despite having $300 million and $20 million in sales respectively. Most companies in the industry were valued at $1 million per employee, and this company had 40. However, NASDAQ had just dropped about 20 percent (April, 2000), and voices predicting the end of the tech stocks' ride were appearing daily in the press.

Therefore, the context was that the potential existed to sell the company soon for a substantial return to one of its competitors. However, if the market turned in a big way, the potential valuation could come screaming down. The business would not fail, as it was choosing its customers and was already at cash flow break-even, but the investors might get stuck as minority shareholders if it became difficult to sell.

In this case, a deal structure with a note convertible to common shares would allow the investors to convert if the company was sold or went public, thus getting their upside. Alternatively, they could call the note after two years if the company was not able to exit but was generating positive cash flow. The deal structure can impact the attractiveness of an investment opportunity by addressing contextual or other factors.

Challenges with the business opportunity, or the time-frame, can sometimes be addressed by finding a key member of management or an active angel who can help the company to move much faster through active use of their network.

Between people, opportunity, deal and context, there are a variety of multi-relational issues and opportunities. Invest in companies that have outstanding elements or at least good combinations and you will hit some winners.

Ten tips for finding money

1. **No one is given capital because of their pretty blue eyes.**
   The project should have clear, distinct concepts. And the business plan should include intelligible, intelligent finance planning for at least three years to come, as well as a worst-case scenario in the event that the project cannot be developed as planned.
2. **Euphoria is out of place**.
   When making your plans, always remember that realization takes much longer and costs much more than you think.
3. **Your first presentation to a potential investor will always differ greatly from the tenth presentation.**
   So it makes good sense to present your project first to someone from whom you don't mind hearing 'no' as an answer. The motto is 'learning by doing'.
4. **It is a good idea to have a targeted plan.**
   But don't limit your frame of reference. Be flexible. Sometimes someone you least expected will offer you help. The more potential investors and customers who know about you, the greater the chances that you will find the right partner.
5. **Even when a presentation or an interview turns out to be tougher than you ever imagined, don't despair.**
   It is always difficult to get the ball rolling. But once it happens, it can set off an avalanche.

6. **Young entrepreneurs who are not willing to give up some of their shares to potential financiers who want to participate in the company will seldom be successful.**
   Because it is a fact: whoever invests wants to have a say in the company.
7. **Be very, very careful with finance companies that make great promises but first want to cash in.**
   The finance business is teeming with dubious individuals who are much better at taking than giving.
8. **Publishing information** about your project in newspapers or magazines not only makes it known, but often increases financiers' willingness to invest in your company - and it attracts new customers. Be sure you comply with government requirements regarding the solicitation of funds if you do this.
9. **Co-operation** in the form of a joint venture, for example, is a good way to realize your project together with another company.
10. **If you give up, it indicates either that you were not competent or the project was neither ripe nor well-developed**. An entrepreneur can be recognized by his ability to solve a problem, to find yet another way of reaching his goal.

Investment documentation explained

A number of documents may be required for different reasons during the investment process. These documents are:

Business plan – Described in detail in Chapter 2 of this book.
Information Memorandum (IM) – This document is often produced to clearly define what has been stated by the owners of the business about the business. It is designed to disclose all risks involved in the venture for the purpose of protecting both the investor and the directors of the company. It is the agreement that is acknowledged when an investor subscribes for shares in your venture. Legal advice is generally required to develop this document for any venture.
Shareholders' agreement – The legal document providing protection to shareholders and setting out the rules for key areas of business decisions and controls. This is described in Chapter 17.
Investment summary – This short document of generally two pages in length and is used to attract investors to a presentation or to request an information memorandum.
Bylaws – Bylaws exist for each and every registered company. Bylaws are a list of rules that govern the running of a company. They outline the framework for adhering to the requirements of the Corporations Act and ensures that some very basic decisions have been made and are in place when a company is formed.
Modified Bylaws – Bylaws modified in some way. The term "modified bylaws" generally refers to bylaws that has been changed to include protection for early-stage minority investors during the early days of a venture. This is discussed further in Chapter 17.

A questionnaire for angels and potential angels

Setting your investment criteria

Questions to ask yourself before starting the search process:

- Overall, how willing am I to invest in Angel deals?
- How many angel investments do I want to make in total? How much money am I willing to risk per deal?
- In what industry sector(s) am I most experienced and most comfortable investing?
- How far am I willing to travel to help my investment?
- Am I more comfortable investing with others, or by myself?
- Realistically, what potential returns am I looking for in an investment deal?
- What basic characteristics am I looking for in the entrepreneur? The product? The target market? The overall business plan?
- Which issues are most important to me, and which am I willing to compromise on?

Starting your search

- Which of my personal friends or business associates might have the network contacts to help me find some potentially attractive angel opportunities?
- Should I try to join an angel syndicate so that I can co-invest with others?
- What do other investors in the area have to say about these services?
- What aspects of the search do I really need help and guidance with?
- Rather than waiting to find a suitable early-stage firm, are there any impressive young ventures in the area that I may want to approach with an unsolicited offer for funding?

Screening investment opportunities

- Who referred this opportunity to me? Do I fully trust their recommendations?
- Do I understand and have experience in this industry sector?
- What makes this investment opportunity unique among all the others?
- What kind of investment return can I realistically expect to receive?
- How much money are the entrepreneurs looking for? How much equity are they willing to surrender in return?
- What are the most likely exit routes for this investment opportunity?
- Overall, does this investment opportunity fit well with my investment criteria?

5

Is Your Venture Team Investment Ready?

Innovative ventures that are looking for sizeable amounts of capital need to be 'Investment Ready'. This means that your team members have moved themselves into a position where they are capable of immediately using the investment to significantly progress the innovation and the business.

To attract an investor, your innovative venture needs to present the investor with significant benefits to be gained from making an investment.

Having your business ready for the introduction of an external investor (i.e. Investor Readiness) requires the following:

1. Be prepared to give (sell) a realistic amount of ownership in your innovative venture
2. Separate your team's personal affairs from those of the business.
3. Maintain at least a minimum set of accounting records and be capable of generating a detailed report on these accounts within one week of the end of each month
4. Be honest with the investor with regard to those weaknesses in the business that your team would like the investor, and their funds, to address (e.g. a significant gap in management expertise, help in establishing export markets)
5. Tell the potential investor how you intend working with them to achieve a beneficial result for the business
6. Prepare a business plan detailing how your team thinks the business can operate. Specifically:
    - What it can achieve over the next two or three years
    - Ensure it contains a story that will be attractive to the investor
    - Remember that your investor needs to see that the value of their investment of time and money will increase in the medium-to long-term

- Make sure that any additional needs for capital during the next few years are shown in the plan, even if your team are not wanting to raise additional capital at this time
- Be realistic! - are the dreams of your venture team really achievable if sufficient money is provided?

Typically, having your innovative venture "Investor Ready" is applicable to smaller businesses or those businesses that are young and have the potential for growth. Remember, if your innovative venture is not able to achieve significant growth it is not normally going to be attractive to an investor.

The key aspects of becoming investor ready

Identifying the precise purpose of the investment - for example:
- To commercialize intellectual property or concept
- To provide a mechanism for existing management to purchase the business from its current owners
- To invest in additional plant and machinery
- To expand the business into other geographic regions
- To restructure the business to improve profitability

You should be able to identify:
- The products and services of your team's innovative venture
- Their competitive advantage
- The market or markets that your innovative venture is able to capture
- The types of customers that your team expect to attract
- The reasons that customers will wish to purchase your products in preference to the competition
- Your competition and competitors
- The way in which your team intend to sell or distribute your innovative products and services
- The distribution channels currently in place and the future requirements
- The growth potential for your team's innovative venture market(s)
- Your innovative venture's ability to grow within those markets
- The additional development needed in both the short and medium-term

Preparation for being investment ready

In order to sell your innovative venture to potential investors you will need to have clearly identified the direction the commercialization of your innovation intends taking, and to have identified the strengths, weaknesses, opportunities and threats facing your business, as well as trends in your market place and industry, together with a strategy for growth and expansion. Some costs will be incurred in providing basic information to potential investors or angels.

Some key areas for consideration are:

Planning

1. Strategic Plan. Your team will need to have a documented strategic plan for the business projecting three to five years out, clearly outlining the vision and growth aspirations of the business, your mission statement and clearly identified critical success factors
2. A workable business plan detailing the implementation timetable to achieve the goals set out in the strategic plan
3. A written investment proposal
4. Identified exit strategies for investors and possibly existing business owners
5. Be prepared to communicate your business direction and vision (strategic plan) concisely, both in writing and verbally. Your team may find a powerpoint presentation useful

Financial

1. Your team needs to be able to demonstrate your capital requirements, and how you will be able to service that debt, now and in the future. You will need a well presented long-term financial plan including sales and expense projections, financial resource requirements and cash flows
2. Up-to-date and audited accounts for the previous three years (if available.) If less than two years, interim accounts should also be prepared
3. Analysis and commentary on the accounts should be prepared explaining past performance
4. Up to date (third party) valuations of your plant and equipment/ intellectual property such as patents, licenses, copyrights, design registration etc. This may be particularly applicable to high technology businesses
5. An audit trail - potential investors will want to carry out due diligence on your business. Your accounts and other documentation should have a clear trail which can be traced and verified by a third party
6. Separation of private and business affairs. All personal expenses, not business related must not be put through the business (e.g. children's school expenses, extra motor vehicles)

Business management

An investor or angel will be interested to see first-hand your management style and will look for evidence of a systematic and methodical approach to business management. Some indicators include:
- Benchmarks and efficiency standard
- A detailed plan by month for the next 12 months of operation
- Regular management reports and graphs monitoring business activity and progress
- Use of Industry standards as a guide/comparison for business performance
- An organization chart and job descriptions
- A training and staff developing plan should also be prepared detailing staff growth to meet demands of the expanding business
- Effective use of external advisers such as accountants, mentors and consultants

The market

- A market analysis detailing market research, product growth areas and associated distribution channels
- A clear and demonstrable unique selling point for your product or Service

Angel investors are less influenced by exciting technology than by actual demonstrations of commercial market viability. When presenting to an investor, clear and concise market information is required, including:
- Current sales figures (if trading)
- Who is the target market? - your key customer groups
- Potential market size - domestic and export
- Anticipated market share - domestic and export
- Proposed distribution channels
- Competitor analysis

Your venture team must be able to support these figures with sources and substantiation.

Personnel

Your team members will need to sell themselves and their management skills to potential investors before you sell your innovative ideas. As stated before, investors as a rule invest in the people rather than the business. Some of the personal attributes they will look for include:
- Ability to delegate
- Ability to listen to other people
- Ability to work with a cross-section of people from unskilled staff through to professional advisers
- Realistic self assessment of your own skills and abilities
- You will need to demonstrate an understanding of the business environment you operate in and factors which may affect your market place now and in the future

Further you will probably need to reconsider the role of your team in the business. As a business grows and employs more staff the business owners / shareholders will need to reassess their role. They must migrate from being responsible for everything within the business to being able to delegate responsibility and manage staff. Part of this process is a self assessment of their own skill-set to identify strengths and weaknesses.

Skills can be broadly broken down into these headings:

Planning. Managers at all levels of an organization need to plan, organize, lead, and control. There are, however, differences among managers in the amount of time they devote to each of these activities. Some of these differences will depend on the kind of organization the manager works for and the type of job the manager has.

Technical. Technical skill is the ability to use the tools, procedures, or techniques of a specialized field. The manager needs enough technical skill to accomplish the mechanics of the particular job they are responsible for.

Human. Human skill is the ability to work with, understand, and motivate other people, either as individuals or as groups. Managers need enough of this human relations skill to be able to participate effectively in and lead groups.

Conceptual. Conceptual skill is the mental ability to co-ordinate and integrate all of the organization's interests and activities. It involves the manager's ability to see the organization as a whole and to understand how its parts depend on each other. It also involves the manager's ability to understand how a change in any given part can affect the whole organization.

The business founder(s) must be able to recognize their strengths as well as shortcomings and identify staff and management requirements accordingly. An equity investor, angel or venture capitalist, will be able to assist with the division of responsibility and make sure your skills are utilized efficiently for the benefit of the business.

An organization chart with associated job descriptions, including the business owners, are important tools in ensuring controlled business growth and expansion.

Excitement and Stress
The founder of Visyboard, the late Leon Pratt (died: 1969), is well remembered for the sound and basic advice he offered to people running any type of business, 'Do not allow expenses to exceed income, collect debts, and look after your best customers and employees.'

Leon's son, Richard says, '*Change always brings with it two conflicting sensations. One is excitement. The other is stress ... Most people can choose whether they want to be mostly excited by change or stressed by it.*'

Ten tips for being investment ready

1. Develop passion, vision and purpose for your innovation project
2. Develop a team to assist you
3. Make sure you have a potential customer and include them in your team
4. Build relationships around your team
5. Make some progress every day - the leaps will not come easily
6. Listen to advice, but also be guided by your intuition
7. Avoid negative people - they will drag you down and slow progress
8. Be prepared to make tough decisions, don't be indecisive and stick by your decisions
9. Get prototypes to the market place and keep making continual improvements
10. Endeavor to make the world a better place with your project

Five big mistakes

1. Expecting your investor to take all the risks
2. Being obsessed with secrecy - caution is important, but you have to trust somebody
3. Expecting the world to beat a path to your door - it won't
4. Relying on money to solve everything - it won't
5. Not using the internet as a tool

Success is the progressive realization of worthwhile pre-determined personal goals. No one else can succeed for you. What are your goals?

What special skills do you need to start and succeed in a new innovative venture? In the formative years of a new innovative venture the leadership skills of; creativity, innovation, finance and promotion are required in generous measure.

Is your team investment ready? - a simple exercise

Imagine that a stranger approaches your team and asks if they can buy into your innovation venture. The stranger asks your team to prepare a profile of your business and the positive things it has to offer. What will your team tell, about themselves and your innovation venture?

Remember, the more your team have to offer, the higher the price you can ask.

What personal things would your team list?

- Experience
- Qualifications
- Expertise
- Recognition

What business attributes?

- Goods
- Improvements
- Services
- Profitability
- Market share

What opportunities do you offer? Are they unique?

- Concepts
- Products
- What are your goals?

6

Dealing with Investors

How are proposals evaluated by angels?

Typically three levels of evaluation and screening exist for a new proposal.

Initial

Highly informal, usually by phone or letter and sufficient to disqualify 80- 90 percent of these initial proposals. Often conducted by others or through pitch sessions such as the Founders Forum.

Secondary

The real scrutiny starts here. Some angels require an applicant to complete questionnaires covering the technology, the product, the market and personal histories and finances. They will then check with the person's associates, past employers, lawyers, accountants, suppliers, customers, dealers, competitors and the competitors' customers. Perhaps 25-50 percent of the projects submitted pass from those that manage to get to this stage.

Final screening

Usually a time delay of 6-12 weeks to conduct 'a market survey'. Often such surveys do not occur at all, but instead the angel or investor will use this time to observe the venture team performing under a range of circumstances, as well as relying on their business and technical contacts for feed-back, in assessing the team. They may also commission an independent consultant to appraise the proposal.

In spite of all the above a great deal of irrationality runs through the investment policies of many individuals. Such things as personality conflict can cause the rejection of a very good venture.

Similarly, if an investor likes the entrepreneurial team, he or she may overlook much that would ordinarily call for the rejection of a proposal.

It should be recognized that the vast majority of new businesses are not appropriate candidates for angel investors - although many would like to think they are.

Presenting to angel investors

Angel investors come from all walks of life. Many happen to be interested in investing because they recently had a windfall and many are simply looking for an opportunity to take a small piece of their portfolio to invest in something a little more exciting.

Angels invest for a number of reasons:
1. To secure an extraordinary return on investment commensurable for the risk they take.
2. To be involved in an exciting venture that is of interest to them.
3. To support young entrepreneurs with talent and potential.

Item 1 is generally the most significant reason and this should always be assumed to be the key reason.

An investors' confidence/motivation to invest is a function of one or more of the following:
1. An intimate knowledge and/or experience in the industry.
2. A desire to be involved in generating a success.
3. A confidence in others invested or investing in the venture.
4. A desire not to miss out on the opportunity.

Once you have one or two credible investors involved and invested, items three and four above become very important.

In the previous chapter we dealt with items including planning, management, personnel, marketing and finance. Obviously you will need to present these components in summarized manner as appropriate for your venture. Accompanying documentation will need to be available to show the potential investors that you are indeed investment ready.

The confidentiality agreement

Most angels will not generally sign confidentiality agreements. This is not because they intend to steal ideas, but because they see so many deals that it is impossible for them to remember what they can or cannot disclose in future conversations. This does become a real risk for them and they would simply prefer not to expose themselves.

Generally angels will sign a confidentiality agreement if they are sufficiently interested.

If you have a venture that would benefit from a confidentially agreement being signed then ask for it and make a reasonable effort to secure it. Even if the investor refuses to sign, they at least realize that you are somewhat serious about your intellectual property. A sample of a simple confidentially agreement that has stood the test of time is included in the appendices of this book.

Meeting strategy

Every meeting must have a strategy and preferred outcome. In the first meeting the following objectives should be secured:

1. If appropriate have the confidentially agreement signed
2. Present the venture concept simply, repeatedly and concisely
3. Cover the basic items:
   - Product
   - Market
   - Team
   - Finances
   - Exit Strategy
   - Offer
4. Close with "Are you interested in seeing more, I'd like to invite you to another meeting if this is of interest to you. I have quite a bit we have not been able to share with you. At the end of the second meeting, I expect an answer from you regarding your investment in the our company. We need to allow you enough time to work through the investment potential and to conduct some basic due diligence. Can we set a time for the next meeting now?"
5. "Any further questions? If you were to invest, how much and under what circumstances?" Here we are seeking investment amount, potential director/advisory position, reporting requirements, etc.
6. If the answer is no then find out why

In the second meeting, the following objectives should be secured:

1. Start with "Are there any questions regarding the information we provided you last week?"
2. Same as first meeting
3. Any further questions?
4. Address any special circumstances identified from the previous meeting regarding investment
5. Close with "Are you interested in investing now? If so, how much? Please sign here?"
6. If the answer is no then find out why

The strategy for these meetings is important. It's also important to be prepared for any questions at any time during these meetings.

The following is a list of documents, where appropriate, that should be available for each meeting for viewing:

1. Business Planning
   - Strategic plan
   - Business plan
   - Information memorandum
2. Product
   - Product development plan
   - Product overview
   - Liability and warranty statements
   - Literature
   - IP portfolio
   - Press reviews

3. Marketing
   - Marketing Plan
   - Press releases
   - Past/sample advertising
   - Past articles
   - White papers
   - Customer lists
   - Testimonials
4. Legal
   - Directors minutes and attachments
   - Register of directors
   - Shareholder Register
   - Constitution
   - Contracts and agreements
   - Deeds of IP transfer from entrepreneur
   - Confidentiality agreements
   - CEO and staff employment contracts
5. Finance
   - Profit & loss
   - Balance sheet
   - Past accounting reports
   - Bank statement(s)
6. Sales
   - Sales process plan
   - Sales history

How are proposals evaluated by angels?

The angel will want to undertake a comprehensive review and due diligence study of the innovative venture. The potential investor will want to carry out a number of steps, which may include:

1. **Identifying suitable matches -** Is there a synergy between the skills and experience of the angel and the innovative venture?
2. **A review of the business plan and investment proposal -** Does the venture team really understand all the aspects of commercializing the venture and is it capable of taking the venture to commercialization?
3. **Meeting with the venture team -** If the investor is interested both parties usually meet informally to discuss the innovative venture and potential investor involvement.
4. **Commencing due diligence -** If both parties see some potential, the investor will start initial investigation on the innovative venture and the marketplace, including:
   - A visit to the premises and possibly meet all of the venture team
   - Accounting review. Business accounts and documents reviewed by third party accountant/solicitor
   - Market research. Undertaking market research to confirm business projections
   - Researching products and competitors
   - Substantiation of business valuation and Intellectual Property

5. **Finalize negotiations -** After extensive review of the innovative venture the investor will prepare a letter of offer to confirm the structure of the deal. Once terms have been agreed by both parties the deal can be completed.
6. **Completion of due diligence**
7. **Shareholders' agreement –** Needs to be drawn up for settlement

Angels often look past the business to the business owner. It is important that both parties respect each other's opinions and can form a good working relationship.
The angel will put considerable emphasis on the skills and attributes of the business owner as well as the fundamentals of the business itself.

Securing commitment from the investor

Your team should not rush into a financial arrangement with a potential investor without due consideration. Dealing with an equity investor is very different to dealing with a debt provider such as a bank.

The innovative venture team should establish from the early negotiation stage what, if anything, the investor can add to the business apart from cash. Through the initial meeting process the innovative venture team should be able to identify what benefits the investor can contribute to business growth.

The innovative venture team should undertake due diligence on the potential investor. Key areas that the business owner should confirm or substantiate are:
1. The investor's qualifications, past work and business history (a resume). Are skills and experience relevant to your business. Are the investor's skills "specialized" or "transferable"?
2. Details of other investments in unlisted companies and details of respective business management. Your team should speak to previous business partners if there are any concerns about dealing with the investor.
3. A clear explanation of the benefits the investor can provide to the business including: skills, market / industry contacts and the extent of possible future investment.
4. Written confirmation from the investor of risk and return perceptions of the investment. It is important that both parties are aware of each other's risk perceptions, possible weaknesses in the innovative venture and possible remedial action.
5. Expectation of their future role in the business, possibly even a "position description" to avoid any confusion. This is a very useful tool for assigning responsibility and accountability within the innovative venture team.
6. Investor management and financial reporting requirements (e.g. weekly cash-flows, monthly accounts) particularly if the investor plans to have a "hands-off" involvement with the business.
7. A suitable well-defined exit strategy from the investment and the anticipated timeframe. This should be discussed at a fairly early stage in the negotiations to make sure both parties are in general agreement.

In addition to these points it is important for the innovative venture team to come to terms with the fact that there will be another person involved in the ownership and possibly management of the business. It is critical that all parties understand the ramifications of entering into this type of investment arrangement.

Expected returns

As a guideline the table below compares the earning rate of various investments to the "risk-free" bond rate.

	Return - multiple Investment of Bond rate
• Top 100 Listed Shares	1.5 times
• Smaller Listed	2 times
• Unlisted - profitable	3 times
• Unlisted - little/no profit history	4 times
• Start-up / early stage	6-8 times

Early-stage investors will seek a return of between 40 to 50 percent p.a. compared to a bond rate of six percent p.a.

Expectations of returns of this nature may seem high and even unrealistic to some innovative venture teams, but the investor will quickly point out that inevitably some investments are bombs and disasters which are written off, and thus require high returns from other investments.

Many investors will invest in say, 10 projects, expecting one, two or three to actually lose money, three of four to break even and the other three or four to pay handsome dividends.

Due diligence

Potential investors will look at your past record of achievements, and be greatly influenced by your team's track record. They will look at your team's relevant industry experience - in many cases formal qualifications will be secondary. They will look at your systems and procedures, accounting records and management information systems - are they based on real-time, do they accurately monitor the performance of the business?

Many small business proprietors have bruised egos by the time they are ready to talk to potential investors such as angels, resulting from being knocked back by banks and perhaps venture capitalists. A typical investor will expect a clear and concise business plan which will work and which is capable of being implemented. The most important consideration of all to most potential investors is the ability to work with the current venture team. In the majority of cases the potential investors are more interested in investing in the people rather than the idea or concept.

An investors assessment of how entrepreneur ego and loss of control issues will affect their investment will often make or break a deal. Often, the entrepreneur will not find out the truth about why the investment was not considered. An inflexible entrepreneur not willing to move aside in the future for the benefit of the company will rarely gain investment from sophisticated angel investors. Potential investors will expect you to understand their perspective of risk and return.

Communicating with your angel

You will need to take some steps to set up a feedback and communication system with your angel. This may include:
1. Periodic executive meetings to review progress and what the next goal priorities should be.

2. Organizational meetings in which the team and/or angel meets, on a systematic planned basis, with employees in order to keep apprised of the state of progress.
3. Renewal conferences. As an example a six monthly planning meeting to examine the people involved, their personal and company priorities, new forces in the environment, forthcoming planning issues, what has happened in their working relationships and other issues for review.
4. Performance review on a systematic, goal directed basis.
5. Feedback from outside parties e.g. accountant and customer satisfaction surveys.

What are some businesses that angels have backed?

There is no limit to when it comes to imagination and scope in regard to the types of businesses that entrepreneurial business owners seek angels to help fund and grow - with and without success. For example:

- A computer strategy game
- A manufacturer of an 'everlasting urn' - a small container with a plaque for holding the ashes from a cremation
- A new version of the traditional hop-scotch game
- A mobile tool box and work bench
- Computer software for scheduling and tracking activities of any type
- An E.E.G. test indicating exposure to chemicals
- A cement smoothing machine, the principles of which the entrepreneur 'could not possibly explain in one hour'
- A robotic grass painting device for golf course and other sports event logos
- Multimedia development for a company established for 30 years
- The establishment of a mail processing and data base company
- Recreational products for the disabled and elderly
- A marine safety tracking system
- A trailer lock
- Educational software focusing on literacy and numeracy
- A home security company
- A motorized hand trolley
- A fruit-processing co-operative with more than 60 members
- And of course many of the high technology companies which have listed on the stock exchange at huge premiums in recent years.

Preparing an investment summary

A well-prepared investee will take the time, care and trouble to prepare an investment summary. You can prepare an investment summary by following the outline below. A summary should be no more than two pages in length and should excite the investor enough to want to read your full proposal and business plan.

Investment proposal XYZ Pty Ltd

1. Background
XYZ Pty Ltd was established in July 2008 by Jim Smith and Michael Jones (50 percent partners and shareholders) to commercialize a patented and commercially proven lockable, sliding door system. The system has been developed over a number of years by the partners. Turnover last year was

$636,000. A copy of last year's accounts are attached. The business proprietors have strong industry backgrounds complemented by relevant tertiary education and professional qualifications.

Brief CV's are attached.

2. The business
The sliding door system was developed in response to a strong and growing market demand for a lockable, sliding door system to combat current high levels of break-ins.

The company's objectives are to:
1. Provide high quality, branded products and services to consumers through a network of national dealers at a competitive price
2. Provide a comprehensive range of marketing support, training for dealers and installers, ensuring distribution channels deliver maximum customer satisfaction
3. Increase market share as a leading industry innovator. The company has achieved several major milestones over the past 12 months:
   - Received a major export order
   - A major builder has placed a two-year contract for supply of all its sliding doors
   - Won second prize in the local Chamber of Commerce awards for excellence
   - Negotiated direct supply of raw materials from the manufacturer, enabling significant cost savings

3. Marketing strategy
Marketing activity is segmented into new home supply and installation market and the renovation/restoration market.
1. New Home Supply. To both state, national and overseas builders of project homes and housing estates
2. The renovation/restoration market. The product continues to make major gains in this market

4. Investment proposal
An equity position of 40 percent is now on offer for an investment of $375,000.

Funds will be used as follows:

$250,000   To expand production capacity to meet local and export demand
(we have a need to increase production capacity by 50 percent within nine months to meet orders)

$125,000   To accelerate commercialization of new products currently in research and development stage and bring to market within 12 months

The investment offers short-term dividend return and strong capital growth in the long term.

5. Cash-flow projections

	08/09	09/10	10/11

Sales ($ 000's)	650	950	1,500
GP %	25%	30%	33%
EBIT ($000's)	58	145	225

6. Exit mechanism

After a three year period, the current shareholders will undertake to buy back part or all of the incoming shareholder/ investor at an agreed earnings multiple. If a shareholder/investor wishes to stay in the company, a public listing is planned in five to six years.

An excellent format for a one page summary is provided in the following example for Seasafe, a company who received funding in 2007 through membership of the Apollo 13 and Brisbane Angels, angels groups based in Queensland. The format is provided through the AngelSoft online system used by all Angels Institute members.

The sample below was printed with the kind permission of Seasafe Pty Ltd. This is a standard format accepted by Angels Institute and other angel group members using the Angelsoft deal management system.

Seasafe Pty Ltd

Deal Room Email: █████████████████

Business Summary: Seasafe Pty Ltd is a technology development company with a clear brief to develop internationally unique and sustainable leading edge solutions for substantiated global growth markets.Our company consistently looks to address and exploit specifically identified global markets and to develop technology which is unrivalled technologically, in price and performance.We have developed high volume, high margin technology with no direct competition.

Management: Management experience overview Lee Waters CEO - Industrial Measurement & Control Tecnician, Inventor & successfull business founder & owner 20 yrs. John Dempsey Director - Accountant, Tax Agent, Auditor in Public Practice & Chartered Secretary.Degrees in accounting & financial management & Agricultural Economics. Director of companies , own accounting practice. Jim Elder Director - ex-Deputy Premier, State Minister,international businesman.

Customer Problem: International Search & Rescue & maritime community has been desperate for an affordable 'localised' SAR system offering instant response.Current satellite systems are inaccurate and may take hours to respond.

Product/Services: We have developed an affordable, accurate & technological superior solution to compliment and supplement current systems. We have directly addressed and overcome perceived inadequacies in existing technologies. We offer an immediate response to emergency situations at the TIME & PLACE they ocurr. Saving time saves lives. Our system does not rely on a national or international co-ordination centre to initiate a (delayed) response to an incident.

Target Market: Global market growing at an estimated 15 to 20% per annum. Marine: Recreational boating and fishing, Charter operators, Scuba diving, Yacht charters, Competitive yachting, Any water sports activity, OEM Boat Manufacturers, Commercial fishing/diving, Search and rescue authorities, Defence Forces/Navy, Merchant Navy, oil/gas platform workers, Aircraft life jackets life rafts, Extensive non-marine land based market.

Customers: Global maritime community. Aus Coast Guard & VMR, Royal Aus Navy, US Customs & Border Protection, US Coast Guard, US fisheries, Intl Dive Industry, Fishing fleets, National Parks (hikers/bushwalkers)

Sales/Marketing Strategy: Achieved some National and International marketing exposure through :New Inventors" show. Several press articles and magazine articles. Marketing through website and intend to offer on-line sales. Further marketing through appropriate media advertising and exhibitions.Distribution model is based on one exclusive (subject to performance) national distributor. They will distribute through network of 2500 retail outlets.Maintain customer database.

Company Profile:
URL: australiantrackingsystems.com
Industry: Telecommunications
Employees: 1
Founded: 02/04/2004

Contact:
Lee Waters
lee@australiantrackingsystems.com
w 07 3488 2622
c 0438 183 735
f 07 3488 2633

Financial Information:
Funding Stage: Prototype Ready
Previous Capital: $400000
Monthly Burn Rate: $20000
Pre-Money Valuation: $1500000
Capital Seeking: $150000

Management:
Lee Waters, Mr.
John Dempsey, Mr.
Jim Elder, Hon.

Advisors:
Lawyer: Minter Ellison
Accountant: John Dempsey

Investors:
████████
████████

Referred By:
████████

Business Model: Primary business model is based on continuing R & D of leading & unparalled technology. Our focus is innovation and development of new technology. We would outsource manufacture and ditribution.

Competitors: Seasafe is unique and has no direct competitors. In the SAR industry the alternate technology is EPIRBS (electronic positioning indicating radio beacon) which is reliant on COSPAR SARSAT satellite system for transmission and response through Canberra. EPIRBs operating on 121.5 MHZ freq will be useless from 2009 when the system is disbanded. users will have to upgrade to expensive 406 MHZ EPIRB. This provides an excellent opportunity for us.

Competitive Advantage: Primary barrier to entry is technological. Have Australian and international prov patents. Competitors would require alternative technology to compete. Additional barrier is the support of Aus SAR authorities.

Seasafe Pty Ltd 9 Lockitt Place Ormiston, QLD 4160 AUS	Financials*	2005	2006	2007	2008	2009	2010
	Revenues	$0	$0	$504	$3517	$6945	$9028
	Expenditures	$0	$100	$341	$1857	$3602	$4142
	Net	$0	$(100)	$163	$1660	$3343	$4886

* In Thousands (000)

Managing the change resulting from investment

Change is inevitable if an angel invests in your team's innovative venture (and inevitable even if your business expands without the aid of an angel). As manager your team will have to introduce change. To avoid any disruption your team will have to be sure that your workers recognize that the change is needed and that the proposed change is the right change.

This will require advance discussion with them to reassure them regarding the expected effects of the change and to seek their support and cooperation in introducing it. An instinctive response to change is, 'What's in it for me?' and the answer for this has to be convincing.

Resistance to change can be triggered by many fears, e.g. fear of:
- Redundancy
- Loss of security
- Disorganization
- Loss of status
- Inability to cope
- Loss of existing relationships
- Or by general apathy or a feeling of denial of existing expectations. The reasons are many.

People usually cooperate if they feel they will:
- Gain benefit
- Avoid loss
- Receive acceptable responses to their uncertainties. They may otherwise resist change sometimes even to the point of sabotaging it.
- Gain advantage from the change which outweighs any disadvantages.

One approach to introducing change is to:
- Identify the required outcomes of the change
- Analyze and plan the change procedures
- Discuss the change with those who will be involved
- Gain acceptance of the proposed change
- Check the step-by-step introduction of the change to ensure that it proceeds as planned.
- Follow up to ensure that what was intended has been achieved.
- Probably the most important requirement for continued change is a continued feedback and information system that lets people in the organization know the system status in relation to the desired states.

Working with angels will inevitably involve change. Reactions to change can involve four stages or phases:
1. Denial,
2. Anger,
3. Assessment and
4. Renewal.

To understand change fully, it is also necessary to appreciate the unchanging. In The Devils Dictionary, Ambrose Bierce has an interesting definition of 'fool': *A person who pervades the domain of intellectual speculation and diffuses himself through the channels of moral activity. He is omnific, omniform, omnipercipient, omniscient, omnipotent.*

Executing change
1. **Analyze of urgency.**
2. **Support a strong leader role.**
3. **Line up political sponsorship.**
4. **Craft an implementation plan.**
5. **Develop enabling structures.**
6. **Communicate, involve people and be honest.**
7. **Reinforce and institute change.**

Tips and tricks for investors
Angels count on an annual return of between 40 and 50 percent as a general guide. There is a lot of money to be made by investing in young companies. But the risk is correspondingly high. In the event of failure, the money is gone. Which means that any involvement should be carefully examined beforehand. Taking a close look at all the factors will protect investors from getting caught in an adventure.

Potential for success. Not every investment made by an angel or venture capitalist results in success. Quite the contrary; statistics from the USA indicate that out of an average of 10 companies only one becomes a real success. Two to three result in moderate yield. Another three barely manage to survive.

Consultation. It is important that the young company benefits from advice and assistance, because the founder is often inexperienced in business management. Marketing, sales, auditing supervision and cash-flow management are often the stumbling blocks. That is where the tips and know-how of experienced entrepreneurs and professional experts are worth their weight in gold. In crisis situations it will be up to the financier to motivate young entrepreneurs anew and get the company back on track.

Personality. The character and personality of the founders play a determining role in whether the company succeeds or fails. Look for perseverance, a feeling for business, technological knowledge, marketing skills and honesty. Investment is only advisable when the entrepreneurial team is 100 percent committed to business, invests all its money in it, brings in intellectual property rights for the product in question and can present a realistic business plan.

Degree of innovation. A product or service must have significant, distinct advantages over existing products or services and it must have a market. If the competitive situation has not been clearly examined and it has not been established if this new product or service can be offered at a competitive price, or if it is not obvious how it will be sold or retailed, then proceed with caution.

Having a say. Investors should absolutely guarantee that they have a say in the innovative venture. Clever investors insist on the right of veto for budgetary matters and for strategic management decisions.

The business plan. The innovative venture founding team must be able to show what capital is at hand, what the financial structure has been thus far and any contracts that exist with third parties. If the assessment of financial needs up to the breakthrough point, or the anticipated profits are not realistic, then it is advisable for an investor not to get involved in the project. A basic rule of thumb is, the less a project has been developed, the greater the risk factor.

Knowledge of the industry. It is always advantageous for the investor to be familiar with the branch of the industry in question. And even if there is a business plan, he should make additional investigations of his own and check references, including those about the company founder himself/herself.

People, people, people. We can't say it too often, people make an investment possible. A great invention with huge potential is worthless unless the team can work effectively and efficiently in the commercialization of the product. It's a rare opportunity that succeeds without good people. Investors have become involved in a 'winning' proposition in the past only to find it does not work. These inexperienced investors are generally diluted until someone takes this "amazing opportunity" combines it with the right people and finally gets the venture off the ground. The early investors and the inventor lose a great deal in this process. People, people, people; can't say it enough.

Types of participation. Investment can take the form of participation through subscription to part of the share capital, through profit-oriented loans as well as through convertible bonds or warrant issues, which during or after a specific amount of time can be changed into shares - at conditions agreed upon in advance. Because young entrepreneurs can seldom provide any collateral security, conventional loans are not particularly suitable for financing a company.

The price of shares. When assisting in the foundation of a new company, pay at least the minimal par value of the shares. A fair arrangement is the payment of a premium for know-how, previous work done for patents brought in to the business, etc., which injects additional capital into the new company. In any case, fairness and honesty in any venture is extremely important. If an entrepreneurial team feels you are taking advantage of them, they will hardly feel motivated to develop their company into a turnover treasure.

Yield. Investment in an innovative venture that will be quoted on the stock exchange within a few years is particularly interesting. It is difficult for an investor to get out of his commitment without a trade sale or by going public. Selling a minority participation to third parties reduces the yield to a minimum. It is much more interesting to sell a successful young company in its entirety. In the event that the founding team or the management buy back their shares, capital gains will also be reduced to a moderate level.

The company's value. The determining factor is proved profits, which - depending on risk evaluation - can be multiplied by a factor of from 10 to 20. The result is the value of the company.

A founders checklist:

- **Do you covet security of the crowd?**
- **Do you operate by consensus and committee?**
- **Are you willing to make sacrifices?**
- **Are you comfortable working seven day, 60 - 80 hour weeks?**
- **Are you easily distracted working on special projects?**
- **Are you prepared to do more than your competitors?**
- **Can you make important decisions?**
- **Can you keep your head when those about you are losing theirs?**
- **Can you handle constant rejection and apathy?**

Source:
SECA Swiss Private Equity & Corporate Finance Association, A Founder's Checklist

Can you answer the following angel investor questions?

- What is your exit strategy?

- What are the milestones you are currently targeting? What are key dates?

- Who is the current CEO and do you believe they are the best available?

- If not, how do you plan to get the best CEO to drive your business?

- Has the IP been transferred under contract to the business venture?

- Who is on the board of directors?

- Who signs the checks? Are one signature or two required?

- What limits on spending require board approval?

- What press releases or media coverage have you received?

- Who does you public relations and marketing?

- Have you applied for R & D tax concessions?

- Have you received any grant funding?

- What is the share structure? Who are the shareholders?

- Who has contributed and how much time into the business?

- Who has put how much money into the business?

- What return should I expect from my investment?

- What problems should I know about as an investor in your venture?

- Do you have a policy on customer service?

- Are there any outstanding options in the company?

- Is there any long term debt?

- Are there any claims against the organization or the principals of the venture?

A quick checklist - are you investor ready?

Are you ready to deal with potential investors?

	Yes	No

Planning
- ☐ Do you have a written investment proposal?
- ☐ Can you explain the reasons you wish to raise extra capital?
- ☐ Do you have a strategic plan?
- ☐ Do you have a workable business plan in place?
- ☐ Can you communicate your business direction and vision (strategic plan) concisely, both in writing and verbally?
- ☐ Have you identified critical factors for success?
- ☐ Have you planned several years ahead in summary?
- ☐ Have you projected financial resources requirements?
- ☐ Have you assessed and quantified your growth aspirations?
- ☐ Does your business have a mission statement?
- ☐ Have you identified a possible exit strategy?

Financial
- ☐ Have you assessed and quantified your capital requirements?
- ☐ Do you have your up-to-date accounts on hand?
- ☐ Have you analyzed past performance?
- ☐ Have you prepared a weekly cash flow?
- ☐ Have you checked sales projections?
- ☐ Have you checked expense expectations?
- ☐ Have you decided on profit targets?
- ☐ Have you projected financial resources?
- ☐ Do you have up-to-date valuations of your plant and equipment available?
- ☐ Have you removed all personal finances from the business?

Market
- ☐ What is your Unique Selling Point?
- ☐ Do you have market and competitor analysis?
- ☐ Have you assessed your expansion aspirations?

Business Management
- ☐ Have you set efficiency standards?
- ☐ Have you detailed next year's plan by month?
- ☐ Do you use reports and graphs to control progress?
- ☐ How do you compare against an industry profile?
- ☐ Do you have an organizational chart and job descriptions?

Personal
- ☐ Can you delegate?
- ☐ Are you comfortable working with people who may be smarter than you and who may have more experience and be better educated than you?
- ☐ Have you had a close look at your own skills and abilities?

Exit strategies

Exit strategies are ways in which investors or potential investors and the proprietors will be able to sell out of a business, preferably at a considerable profit, at a time of their choosing.

Potential investors will be most concerned with having an exit strategy in place for any possible eventualities, success, failure or breakeven.

The investor's first preference is to sell the business as a going concern or to list the business on the stock exchange and also to make substantial capital gains in the process.

In the event that the business is not meeting expectations or if the investment sours they will want to assess how they can quit their involvement with your business, with at least as much money as they put in, or by recovering as much as possible.

Investors will ultimately wish to realize the profit in their investment - thus investors may wish to sell for a number of reasons such as; maximizing the return on investment, taking advantage of improved profits and/or pursuing other investment opportunities.

The expectations and some typical exit strategies of investors when quitting or selling out of your business could include:

- Selling their investment, in the later development stages, to another investor
- Selling their investment to take advantage of improved profits
- Selling their investment to pursue other opportunities
- Selling their investment back to original shareholders
- Selling their investment and /or the business to another organization as a take-over target
- Selling the business to the company management in a management buyout
- Floating the company on the stock exchange
- Sale to another venture capital company
- Disposal of the investment and/or the business to another organization in a merger or takeover

A very sound suggestion is to write a detailed exit mechanism clause into any agreements. For instance: After a three year period, the current shareholders will undertake to buy back part or all, of the incoming shareholder at an agreed earnings multiple. If an investor wishes to stay in the company a public listing is planned in five to six years.

Methods of selling the business to meet exit strategies

When an angel or investor reaches the stage of wanting to sell out of a business there are a number of options the investor could use to find a buyer in order to sell their stake, or the complete business.

A public sale by advertising or calling for expressions of interest. This results in a lack of secrecy which some people have a problem with. The advantages are that it usually identifies a number of potential buyers unknown to those wanting to sell.

A targeted sale by short listing potential buyers, preparing an information memorandum and inviting offers. This method encourages competitiveness and helps maintain secrecy. Alternatively you may choose to sell off unprofitable parts of the business and keep the core elements of the business which produce the most profits. Another option might be to sell off assets (e.g. sell the business premises and lease them back) and reinvest the money realized in the business.

Possible downside

By following all of the previous guidelines and recommendations your innovative venture team will be on the right track to a successful and profitable relationship with an investor.

In the event there is a falling out between parties there are various options open. Generally most eventualities will be covered in the shareholders' agreement where all shareholders rights and obligations should be clearly articulated. This document should be prepared by a qualified legal practitioner with commercial experience, particularly in the commercial innovation sector. Each party should have an independent review of the agreement before signing. Ultimate decision making power will rest with the majority shareholder, although there are remedies within the corporations law protecting minority shareholders.

The pros and cons of entrepreneurs

Normal, rational, straightforward people don't build billion-dollar businesses. It takes someone with passion, heart and emotion to do it.

Pros
- They provide the drive, vision and energy behind a company
- They are involved in every facet of the business
- They remain focused on the company's core businesses

Cons
- They have too much control and fail to listen to others
- They often seem to be abrasive
- They do not suffer fools gladly
- Companies can also become vulnerable to their mistakes

Dispute resolution

In the event that an amicable decision cannot be reached, it is often included within the terms of the shareholders' agreement or even respective management position descriptions, that a third party mediator be invited to resolve the dispute. This may be the company accountant, solicitor or business adviser as first choice. If this is not successful a specialist in Alternative Dispute Resolution (ADR) should be engaged. ADR is a rapidly growing option to full-blown legal proceedings. ADR is an extremely progressive "confidential" problem-solving process designed as an alternative to arbitration and litigation.

It is a voluntary process through which disputing parties meet with a "neutral third party" (mediator) who assists them to negotiate their own settlement solution.

Mediation is suited to any dispute in which; time and expense is important, a negotiated settlement is desired, the parties wish to keep the proceedings confidential and tension and emotions are impeding communication.

Your solicitor, or the Law Society should be able to advise you of suitable ADR practitioners.

Ultimately all parties should not lose sight of the fact that they are in business to make money. All parties should only enter into the investment transaction in good faith and with full disclosure.

Business failure

Unfortunately there are no 100 percent guarantees of success in the business world and there is some real risk that the innovative venture may fail or profits may fall way short of expectations. The possibility of an unsuccessful outcome and the consequences of this should be considered up-front and should be discussed openly with the investor. Both angels and venture capitalists have a pragmatic view of the potential losses and will have factored this into their risk - a return analysis of the business. Part of the due diligence process is to look at the "worst case scenario" and see what could be salvaged if the business failed. As the investor usually ranks alongside ordinary shareholders in the event of a business failure they will be keen to maximize any recovery of capital. They will work with banks, creditors and other shareholders to find the best possible outcome. This may be; sale as a going concern (e.g. to a competitor), sale of assets and intellectual property, appoint an administrator/scheme of arrangement with creditors or a wind-up/liquidation. A decision on this course of action must be agreed by the directors.

Why do some innovative businesses fail?

Lack of experience. Not having enough knowledge of the industry. Not knowing how to buy, sell, interact with customers, etc.

Inadequate financial controls. Not having enough money for day-to-day running costs, as well as the purchase of up-to-date machinery, buildings, motor vehicles, etc.

Poor record keeping. Preparing insufficient or unsuitable records which prevent managers from making efficient business decisions.

Insufficient inventory control. Holding too much stock, resulting in funds tied up unnecessarily, or holding stock which has deteriorated or become out of date.

Poor credit control. Giving credit to the wrong people. Not ensuring that people pay accounts on time.

Inadequate marketing. Not being able to advertise, sell and distribute the product or service correctly.

Staff problems. Employing too many staff. Employing unsuitable staff. Poor staff supervision.

Lack of appropriate technology. Failure to use appropriate technology for the type of business may mean the business is not competitive.

Unsuitable location. Not being close to transport facilities or not enough demand for the product in a certain area.

Withdrawal by the owner of too much cash. Thinking that profits are made up of cash, owners take money out of the business too quickly leaving insufficient funds for expansion.

Lack of good corporate governance

Mitigating risk of the business venture and putting in place good protection processes and policies is paramount for any successful company. Good corporate governance can take precious resources and balancing the provision whilst maintaining an efficient operation is not easy. Without good corporate governance understanding a company can take on far more risk than it should.

Summary - proceeding with your Investor

What are some ways in which the potential investor will want to be able to exit the business? Their expectations and exit strategies when quitting or selling out of your business would include:

- Selling their investment, in the later development stages, to another investor
- Selling their investment to take advantage of improved profits
- Selling their investment to pursue other opportunities
- Selling their investment back to the owner
- Selling their investment and/or the business to another organization as a takeover target
- Selling the business to the company management in a management buyout
- Listing the company on a stock exchange.

7

The Negotiation Process

Introduction

Every venture is worth something.

We will look at a couple of scenarios that will provide a rough picture of what may be possible.

Note in the following scenarios, that the situation is overly simplified and that broad assumptions are made. It does not ask the question "Is $100,000 enough to secure the first milestone?" and does not take into account findings of due-diligence or absence or existence of a good business team. It does assume the deal is considered investible and robust but not without risk.

Scenario 1: Great Idea

Bob & Bill decide over a beer that they have the next widget that will make millions. They split it 50/50 with Bob doing the work and Bill investing $25,000 to get the first prototype out the door. They haven't started work but they have planned the process in their minds.

Let's assume that Bob and Bill are good operators who have some good industry knowledge, are educated, are passionate and are willing to work hard and with others in the best interests of the company.

They decide to raise $100,000 that they will need to generate 1000 units of inventory and to provide operational capital for the next six months including a minimal salary for Bill.

Scenario 1 - Valuation 1:

Since Bill has invested $25,000 and Bob will have to work for a few months (or already has) one could assume that the value of the business is $50,000. If this were the case then $100,000 of additional capital would leave Bob & Bill with a 33 percent holding in the company.

Scenario 1 - Valuation 2:

Since the idea has some merit one could argue that it may be worth more. More importantly, the reality is that if the investor wants both Bob and Bill to remain highly motivated, they will need to retain a higher shareholding in the company. Let's value the business at $500,000 and take a 20 percent position for the $100,000 investment.

Scenario 1 – Valuation 3:

Bob and Bill believe the idea is worth a fortune. They are valuing it at $1 million and will not accept anything less. Bob claims it came from many years in the industry and is sure they will raise an additional $2 million in a second round at a higher valuation. This means the $100,000 investment will secure a 10 percent equity position for the investor.

Scenario 1 – Valuation 4:

Bob and Bill have been to an accountant for a formal valuation. They are projecting profits of $15 million in the third year of operations on sales of $35 million. With discounted cash flow calculated and adding a further discount for the risk involved they have come up with a valuation of $5 million. An investment of $100,000 would secure a 2 percent equity position to the investor.

Which deal would an investor accept? What is fair?

Scenario 1 – Discussion of Valuation 1:

If Bob and Bill were of little value to the team, and if the investor is burdened with the job of making the company viable, then it is possible for this deal to be made to make sense. In general, however, based on the assumption that Bob and Bill have proven value and are passionate about the product, it would make little sense for an investor to make such a deal. Bob and Bill would soon be diluted to a less than attractive position in the company and lose interest. The investor could lose all the investment or be forced to invest a great deal of time to develop people to take the company forward. It's hard to imagine many investors would consider such a deal.

Scenario 1 - Discussion of Valuation 2:

It's very difficult to value any deal. Many deals take this form and level with variation from $500,000 to $1 million subject to the detail of the deal. This could become a viable investment if due diligence provided sound basics.

Scenario 1 – Discussion of Valuation 3:

See above.

If $2 million is required to commercialize the deal, it would be imperative that the company must get this funding. Without it the follow-on investment it may be a trap for new investors. The company needs to achieve the pre-set milestones to generate the valuation required to raise these funds. What also often happens is that just because the company has spent the $100,000 well and met the milestones, the next level valuation is not realistic/achievable and the company cannot raise the funds required. In this case the $100,000 should not have been invested.

Scenario 1 – Discussion of Valuation 4:

Accountants generally warn early-stage companies that valuations without existing cash-flow are difficult to believe and are often meaningless to investors. Confidence to accept high valuations is rare among investors although it can be achieved with a particularly strong opportunity with a strong team. A company can be assured that a venture capitalist or a sophisticated angel group will not accept such a valuation easily. In general, something very substantial such as existing cash-flow and/or existing assets would be needed to justify such a valuation under the circumstances provided.

Another way to look at this would be to assume the company already had a marginally profitable early cash-flow. One would clearly argue that the company is more valuable because customers are purchasing product. This is a sign of achievement. If you give this new information to an accountant, you may notice a reduction in the valuation. Why? Because the introduction of history forces the accountant to consider a different set of rules which can point to a lower valuation than the original. Managing this transition can be extremely important.

Scenario 1 - Summary

It is always possible to find a buyer for an investment at a high valuation. The chances of finding an investor go down, however, as the valuation goes up. Dilution is a huge issue for any and all entrepreneurs and needs to be well understood.

Valuations one and four are extremes and will not play out very often. Valuations two and three fit within the general realm of early-stage, hard to value opportunities based on a great idea, early prototypes, patents etc.

Keep in mind that there were two pre-existing valuations in this example. Bob purchased 50 percent of the company for $25,000 valuing the company at $50,000. Bill managed the best deal with 50 percent of the company at a valuation of his time and effort. Finding the middle ground that makes sense is extremely difficult and there is no perfect answer. It is a matter of developing a win-win situation for all parties involved in the negotiation.

Scenario 2: Great Idea with Product and Cashflow

Bob & Bill have progressed. They received the $100,000 investment and spent that money finalizing the first product, manufacturing the first 1000 units and in commencing the commercialization process.

Over the past six months, they managed to sell 500 units at $100 each and still have 500 units in stock at a cost of $50 each. Other costs including development of a new product and sales commissions have put them in a difficult position and they know that they will likely be insolvent within three months if they don't get investment to push out their next product release.

People are raving about the product, but orders are a little more elusive than they had anticipated.

They have decided that they need to raise an additional $500,000 for working capital and to do a production run on their second generation product. Their confidence is building and their forecasts though lower than their original forecasts are also more realistic.

Scenario 2 - Valuation 1:

Since Bill has invested $25,000, Bob has invested time and the first round investor invested $100,000 to produce $25,000 in inventory, one could assume that the value of the business is greater than $100,000. Let's assume the value is $250,000. Raising an additional $500,000 of additional capital would leave Bob, Bill and the new investor with approximately 33 percent of the company.

Scenario 2 - Valuation 2:

With the product being sold, some proven customer value exists. Bob and Bill are still enthusiastic and all are excited about the potential. Let's increase the value the business to include this additional excitement around customer acceptance to a valuation of $1 million and take a 50 percent position for the $500,000 investment.

Scenario 2 – Valuation 3:

Bob and Bill managed to raise the $100,000 at a $1 million valuation in the previous round. They now believe it's worth $2 million because they now have customers and the customers are saying great things about the company. This means the $500,000 investment will secure a 25 percent equity position for the investor.

Scenario 2 – Valuation 4:

Bob and Bill have been to an accountant for a formal valuation. As before, they are projecting profits of $15 million in the third year of operations on sales of $35 million. The accountant is a little shakier this time around, however, they are still willing to maintain the valuation but are not willing to increase it. Bob and Bill have determined that the company must be worth more and have increased the value to $7.5 million anyway. An investment of $500,000 would secure a 6.6 percent equity position to the investor.

Which deal would an investor accept? What is fair?

Scenario 2 - Discussion of Valuation 1: $500,000 for 66 percent on a $750,000 post-investment valuation

Provided Bob and Bill have performed well and remain passionate and hard working, it's difficult to believe this is a fair deal to all involved. Dilution for Bob, Bill and the round one investor is very high and would be unlikely to be accepted if the company were even partially meeting milestones. If an investor did accept such a deal, the investor would have to assume that Bob and Bill would not be well motivated and that they could leave the company.

Scenario 2 - Discussion of Valuation 2: $500,000 for 50 percent on a $1 million post-investment valuation

The deal has only progressed in securing initial customers. This has reduced the risk significantly but has not necessarily increased the valuation. Many deals do take this form.

Scenario 2 – Discussion of Valuation 3: $500,000 for 25 percent on a $2 million post-investment valuation

See above. $1.2 to $2 million could be the range for post-investment valuation dependent on milestones met.

In Scenario 1 it was assumed that $2 million would be required to undertake the required commercialization. If $2 million is required to commercialize the deal, the valuation would be increased to approximately $4.5 million post-investment to allow original investors to maintain reasonable equity positions. Bob and Bill must find someone willing to undertake this investment which includes taking on the risk and potential for this opportunity. An investor must be able to clearly see a return on the investment made. As occurs in many cases, Bob and Bill gave up on raising the $2 million in favor of raising a smaller amount in this scenario.

Was the decision to raise a smaller amount sound? Obviously we don't know all the circumstances. If Bob and Bill had all the ducks in a row, and had developed a team capable of driving the company, then the chances of raising the $2 million would have been increased greatly.

Scenario 2 – Discussion of Valuation 4:

Accountants struggle with valuation of early-stage ventures for good reason. Formulas simply don't fit well. It is possible to find an accountant who will agree with a high valuation. Regardless, it's difficult to raise funds at unreasonable valuations and generally it is only the friends, family and fools (FFF) that fall prey to such investments. Unfortunately FFF do not generally have the money needed to support the venture at a higher levels and many don't succeed as a result.

But wait... with a great team; really great, and a huge opportunity, it can be done, and it can be done successfully. Angels will back a great team with a track record of performance because confidence is increased and risk is reduced.

Scenario 2 - Summary

It was never said that valuation of early-stage companies is easy. It is extremely difficult and a lot has to do with complex elements including the opportunity packaging, personalities, perceptions, market, milestones, timing, team and strategy. Remember that it's hard work, perseverance, teamwork, good thinking and leadership that makes a venture succeed. Be sure that you like and trust the people you get involved. People make the difference.

The "Science" of valuation

The valuation of a company is the price tag offered to investors. Angels don't want to own or control the company hence the need for a good business team to be involved at the outset. Mentors or key personnel need to be attracted to the venture preferably before the angels invest. Attracting good people will also have an effect on dilution before angels become involved.

Developing an estimate of the future value of the company is a useful tool in developing valuation models.

Let's assume a company is determined to be worth $25 million in five years (Terminal Value), and the company seeks to raise $1 million today from investors. Investors seek to secure a 10 times return on investment (ROI) in the five years and therefore they seek to secure $10 million at exit. This means that they must own 40 percent of the company at that time. This would set the pre-money value at $1.5 million. Note that this does not include any allowance for future dilution. If an additional $2 million were required 12 months later, for example, pre-money valuation would drop considerably.

Post-money Valuation = Terminal Value in the nth year/Anticipated ROI in the nth year

= $25 million /10 = $2.5 million

Pre-money Valuation   = Post money Valuation - Investment

= $2.5 million - $1 million = 1.5 million

Venture Structure

Shareholders	Founding	Post Money Ownership			
		Round 1	Round 2	Round 3	Exit
Founders	100%	52%	39%	31%	23%
Mentors/Key Employees		15%	11%	9%	7%
Round 1		33%	25%	20%	15%
Round 2			25%	20%	15%
Round 3				20%	15%
Public Market/Partial trade Sale					25%
	100%	100%	100%	100%	100%
Premoney Valuation		$1,000,000	$3,000,000	$8,000,000	$40,000,000
Invested Capital		$500,000	$1,000,000	$2,000,000	
Post Money Valuation		$1,500,000	$4,000,000	$10,000,000	$40,000,000

Investor Returns

		Round 1	Round 2	Round 3	Total
Years to Exit		5	4	3	
Invested Capital		$500,000	$1,000,000	$2,000,000	$3,500,000
Invested Capital Value at Exit	$9,300,000	$6,000,000	$6,000,000	$6,000,000	$18,000,000
Internal Rate of Return (IRR)		64.4%	56.5%	44.2%	56.7%
Return on Investment (ROI)		12.0	6.0	3.0	5.1

What's wrong with the "science"? There is so much that is not taken into account with the science. Questions that make the science a little too academic at the start-up stage include: Are the projections based on a real market or a brand new market? How were they derived? What funds have been injected to date? And a myriad of other questions.

The valuation of a company is often key to whether the deal proceeds. The relationship between the angel investors and the entrepreneur is established early on. If there is no general agreement early on in the valuation, then it's unlikely that a deal will be made.

The venture structure shown on the previous page shows a typical company structure including both valuation and Internal Rate of Return (IRR) calculations. Investors need to know what the IRR is based on reasonable revenue and profit projections. In the future as cash-flows are established, the valuation is based on achieved earnings rather than projected earnings.

Negotiation 101 – "I've Been Everywhere"

Entertainer Geoff McElhinney, stage name Geoff Mack, was approached by a friend involved in the recording industry, to produce a record based on his travels in the late 50s. One of the six songs chosen for the recording was "The Swagman Rock" which was a simple song with a rock beat that named that he had travelled to.

The record executives made the decision not to call the song "The Swagman Rock". Rock was a relatively new term and they felt strongly that "rock" was just a fad and would not last for much longer and that the name would date as a result. They renamed the song "I've Been Everywhere".

Within a short while, Lucky Starr, a young entertainer who was wooing the teenage girls in 1962 and becoming increasingly popular, took on "I've Been Everywhere" as a challenge, learnt the words and quickly took the song to number one on the top 40 for many weeks.

Geoff's friend and publisher, Johnny Devlin, who encouraged him to publish the songs, decided that it was time to secure his commission on royalties. "Geoff, the normal commission is 20 percent and we need something in writing so I get my piece of the action" said Johnny. Geoff responded, "That's fine with me I'll accept the 50 percent royalty". A little puzzled, Johnny stated, "Geoff, I said 20 percent, not 50 percent". And Geoff replied, "Look, Johnny, you're the one who encouraged me to do this and I want you to be motivated to promote the song anyway, let's stick with 50 percent". The deal was done.

Later in 1963, Hank Snow, a very popular country western singer picked up the song and took it to the top of the national charts.

Since that time Geoff has written over 200 versions of "I've Been Everywhere" for countries and in languages including Japan, Canada, New Zealand, South Africa, Germany, etc. The song has been sung and recorded by Rolf Harris, Lyn Anderson, Willie Nelson, Aunty Jack, Johnny Cash, John Grenell, The Statler Brothers, Glen Campbell, Susan St James, John Denver and Ted Egan to name a few. It has been a remarkable success.

In the late 60s, Johnny decided to sell his publishing company to Belina Music Publishing which was later sold to EMI Music Publishing, now one of the world's leading music publishers. To our knowledge, EMI has only one song on which they receive a 50 percent commission. Geoff McElhinney receives royalties every time "I've Been Everywhere" receives a commercial play. Companies including Choice

Hotels, Coon Cheese and most recently a broadband advertising campaign are but a few of the accounts who have licensed "I've Been Everywhere". The song itself is exceptional, but how much of its incredible success can be attributed to the motivation of the original publisher and now EMI sales representatives. Had Geoff negotiated a better and more traditional deal, how much revenue would he have lost?

(See Appendix 1 - "I've Been Everywhere" lyrics including an amusing email parody)

Incentives that matter – Negotiating with share options

Negotiation involves more than just addressing the needs of raising capital for a venture. If a venture team is clever or fortunate, the funds attracted may come with intelligent advice, contacts and alliances.

Share options provide a valuable currency for the venture to attract both talent and investment. Securing directors, a great CEO, marketing and entrepreneurial talent can be aided greatly by the added value of share options.

Some venture teams fear the dilution effects from issuing share options. The potential dilution that comes with offering equity in the form of share options needs to be well considered in conjunction with the value of the talent or resource being attracted.

Share options will only be exercised (converted to shares) when the value of the options has exceeded the exercise price of the share options.

In the event that the company does not do well, the share option owner gets nothing in return for the effort they have put forward. There is no dilution in this case. If the company does well, shareholders, and share option holders gain as a result. Share options can generate a win-win outcome.

8

Leveraging Government Assistance

Getting to know the government

Working with any government department need not be difficult. It can be very beneficial. If your first encounter with a government body is negative, it is advisable not to judge the government support by this single event. It is possible you approached the wrong person or someone otherwise laboring under a very busy schedule.

Within the government there are some very clever people who can assist you. Take your time and seek out those who can provide you the services you need and don't assume that every government employee knows who you should be talking to.

When you do find the correct person, you will know it and will be pleasantly surprised. The government have made some significant positive changes and will continue to improve their offerings. The support the government provides young entrepreneurs is significant. Your job is to identify what can add value to your venture.

Additional Resources

Universities, Colleges, Incubators and Small Business Centers should also be looked at as sources of assistance. Many programs exist both general and highly focused that can provide significant value in your region. The above listing is far from exhaustive.

9

Stock Exchanges

Introduction

Stock exchange choices include the NYSE, NASDAQ, AMEX and OCTBB as outlined below. Companies seeking exits also consider the UK based Alternative Investments Market (AIM) and the Plus Markets Exchange (PLUS) in discussions at some point. All but the OCTBB and OFEX have merit but are generally out of reach of early-stage ventures with less than $10 million in revenues.

Investors generally seek to invest between 5 percent and 10 percent in a diversified portfolio of early-stage investments. Risking more is not seen to be wise. With their investments, the investors seek those that provide an exit and the stock exchanges can provide such opportunities. As an investor exits a venture the capital that was in the high risk portfolio, these funds are released for additional investment.

The remainder of the investor's funds may be in various allocations including the stock market. Most investors have a good knowledge of stock market trading and therefore can relate to the value of future listings. Many angel investors also keep an eye on potential listings that may require investment as a relatively low risk yet high return opportunity.

In June 1990, the OTCBB began operation, on a pilot basis, as part of important market structure reforms to provide transparency in the OTC equities market. The Penny Stock Reform Act of 1990 mandated the U.S. Securities and Exchange Commission (SEC) to establish an electronic system that met the requirements of Section 17B of the Exchange Act. The system was designed to facilitate the widespread publication of quotation and last-sale information. Since December 1993, firms have been required to report trades in all domestic OTC equity securities through the Automated Confirmation Transaction ServiceSM(ACTSM) within 90 seconds of the transaction.

In April 1997, the SEC approved the operation of the OTCBB on a permanent basis with some modifications, and in May 1997, DPPs became eligible for quotation on the OTCBB. In April 1998, all foreign securities and ADRs that are fully registered with the SEC became eligible for the display of real-time quotes, last-sale prices, and volume information on the OTCBB.

On January 4, 1999, the SEC approved the OTCBB Eligibility Rule. Securities not quoted on the OTCBB as of that date will be required to report their current financial information to the SEC, banking, or insurance regulators in order to meet eligibility requirements. Non-reporting companies whose securities were already quoted on the OTCBB will be granted a grace period to comply with the new requirements. Those companies will be phased in beginning in July 1999 and by June 2000, current financial information about all domestic companies that are quoted on the OTCBB will be publicly available.

About PLUS Markets plc

PLUS Markets plc ("PLUS") is a stock exchange in London. Its quote-driven (market-maker) electronic trading platform currently trades a broad range of securities including full coverage of all London-listed shares like the FTSE 100, and unlisted shares quoted on the AIM and PLUS markets. It is a Recognized Investment Exchange in the UK and a Market Operator under MiFID, authorized to operate both secondary and primary markets. Over 200 small & mid-cap companies are currently on the "PLUS-quoted" market segment, an exchange-regulated market for small and mid-cap companies. It offers an alternative to AIM for high-quality applicants offering the potential for investment returns.

OTC Bulletin Board:

The OTC Bulletin Board® (OTCBB) is a regulated quotation service that displays real-time quotes, last-sale prices, and volume information in over-the-counter (OTC) equity securities. An OTC equity security generally is any equity that is not listed or traded on NASDAQ or a national securities exchange. OTCBB securities include national, regional, and foreign equity issues, warrants, units, American Depositary Receipts (ADRs), and Direct Participation Programs (DPPs).

CHX

The Chicago Stock Exchange was founded May 15, 1882 and is the second most active stock exchange in terms of share and trade volume. The CHX is also the fastest growing exchange providing the strongest force for competition to all U.S. markets. The CHX trades more than 4000 NYSE, AMEX, Nasdaq and CHX-e

Canada's TEX Venture Exchange

TSX Venture Exchange - Serving Canada's public venture equity market, TSX Venture Exchange provides access to capital for companies at the early stages of their growth while offering investors a well-regulated market for making venture investments.

Canadian Trading and Quotation System (CNQ)

CNQ is a stock exchange alternative to traditional stock exchanges where high costs and large capitalization requirements are often barriers to trading in a junior company's securities. Responding to the consolidation of stock exchanges in Canada, CNQ's founders identified the need for a low cost, streamlined stock exchange – with an extremely high standard of disclosure. CNQ's unique market model matches enhanced disclosure and streamlined issuer regulation with leading edge technology to meet the needs and characteristics of emerging companies, their investors and investment dealers. This model, combined with comprehensive regulatory oversight, provides an efficient new marketplace that fosters integrity, transparency and liquidity for trading equity securities.

10

Tips and Checklists for Commercializing Innovation

Tools provided in this chapter serve various purposes. They are designed to gather information and force a structured approach to thinking. With such tools it's often not the results of the process but the process itself that provides the real value from the exercise. Such tools can also be of great value in team discussions and collaborations to extract additional information and encourage lateral thinking.

An Entrepreneur's Checklist

Do you have what it takes? Try this simple quiz and see how you fare. It is generally accepted that a score of less than 100 will require some major personal development on your part, to cope with the demands of your business.

	High	*Low*
1. Do you enjoy making your own decisions?	5 4 3 2 1 0	
2. Are you self reliant?	5 4 3 2 1 0	
3. Do you relish competition?	5 4 3 2 1 0	
4. Are you a self starter?	5 4 3 2 1 0	
5. Do you have will power?	5 4 3 2 1 0	
6. Can you build teams?	5 4 3 2 1 0	
7. Do you plan?	5 4 3 2 1 0	
8. Can you take advice?	5 4 3 2 1 0	
9. Can you adapt to change?	5 4 3 2 1 0	
10. Do you establish schedules of activities?	5 4 3 2 1 0	
11. Do you keep to the skills?	5 4 3 2 1 0	
12. Can you keep others to schedule?	5 4 3 2 1 0	
13. Do you deal with complex issues well?	5 4 3 2 1 0	
14. Can you deal with ambiguity?	5 4 3 2 1 0	
15. Are you capable of adapting to change?	5 4 3 2 1 0	
16. Can you work long hours?	5 4 3 2 1 0	
17. Are you single minded?	5 4 3 2 1 0	
18. Do you have the physical stamina to deal with the project?	5 4 3 2 1 0	
19. Do you have the emotional strength and resilience to handle the strain?	5 4 3 2 1 0	
20. Will you make sacrifices to achieve your goals?	5 4 3 2 1 0	
21. Are you capable of identifying the skills needed for success?	5 4 3 2 1 0	
22. Do you have those skills?	5 4 3 2 1 0	
23. Can you fill in any gaps in your skills from elsewhere?	5 4 3 2 1 0	
24. Can you deal with risk of failure?	5 4 3 2 1 0	
25. Are you skilled at networking?	5 4 3 2 1 0	
26. Can you keep your objectives in view despite distractions?	5 4 3 2 1 0	
27. Do you know your goals?	5 4 3 2 1 0	
28. Can you communicate them to others?	5 4 3 2 1 0	
29. Can you handle several tasks at once?	5 4 3 2 1 0	
30. Do you separate **need to's** from **nice to's?**	5 4 3 2 1 0	

TOTAL

The entrepreneurs checklist provides a series of propositions about individual enterprise. At the core lies a notion that the person is self reliant, and can make personal decisions, enjoys being self reliant and is not intimidated by competition.

Alongside these ought to be the capacity to be a self starter. The enterprising individual does not wait for others to give a lead. This reflects a well formed and strong will.

The attitudes and skills needed by entrepreneurs are seldom as glamorous or exciting as those seen in the movies or those portrayed in popular writing. There needs to be a willingness to roll the sleeves up, take on board the basics and understand the fundamentals.

A product - idea rating device

Does your innovation have what it takes?

Product success requirements	(A) Relative rating weight	(B) Company competence level 0.0 0.1 0.2 0.3 0.4 0.5 0.6 0.7 0.8 0.9 1.0 (A x B)
Company personality and goodwill	0.20	
Marketing	0.20	
Research and development	0.20	
Personnel	0.15	
Finance	0.10	
Production	0.05	
Location and facilities	0.05	
Purchasing and supplies	0.05	
TOTAL	**1.00**	

Rating scale: 0.00 - 0.40 poor, 0.41 - 0.75 fair, 0.76 - 1.00 good
Present minimum acceptance rate: 0.70

Many organizations require their staff to evaluate new product ideas using some type of 'standard format' for later review by a committee. This rating form can be used to address these issues.

The first column lists factors required for a successful launch of the product to the marketplace. The next column shows 'weighting factors' which management may apply to various issues. Thus management believes marketing competence will be very important (0.20), and purchasing and supplies competence will be of minor importance(0.05).

The next task is to rate the organization's degree of competence on each factor on a scale from 0.0 to 1.0.

The final step is to multiply the relative importance of the success requirements by the corresponding levels of organizational competence to obtain a single overall rating of the organization's ability to carry this product successfully to the market place.

Innovation and your organization

	Strongly agree 4	Agree 3	Neutral 2	Strongly disagree 1	Disagree 0	no opinion ?
We have a good track record of innovation by comparison with our competitors and industry						
Our management style does not impede the introduction and development of new products or processes						
In this organization, the forces which favor the preservation of the status quo are balanced by enthusiasm						
It is generally accepted in the organization that there is outstanding creative talent in its ranks						
There are influential people in the organization who support new ideas entirely on their merits						
The management control over activities is not an inhibiting factor for progress						
There are efficient mechanisms for the flow of information necessary for managers to carry out their jobs						
The organization is attempting to stimulate creative thinking through its training programs						
Entrepreneurship is encouraged						
There is a positive attitude and no defeatism where new ideas are concerned						
TOTAL						

When you identify the highest scoring items, this will point to the areas where your organization is strongest in managing innovative performance.
Low scores will suggest weaknesses.

Considerations...................................... Possible actions.............................

Opportunities and threats in launching a new product

OPPORTUNITIES	THREATS
Expand your customer base - more clients • Natural growth • An improved economy • Increased prosperity • Population shifts – positive	**Reduce your customer base - less clients** • Natural attrition • A worsening economy • Reduced prosperity • Population shifts – negative
Improved customer access • Increased range of products • Easier to purchase • New, improved marketing • Improved service and contact	**Reduced, more difficult customer access** • Decreased range of products • Harder to purchase • Old, worsening marketing • Decreased, worsening service and contact
Increased appeal of your products • Advantages over competitors • Market leadership • Other sales approaches	**Decreased appeal of your products** • •Disadvantages over competitors • Loss of market credibility • Competitors sales tactics • Competitors sales strategies
Exploit competitors shortcomings • Opportunities for increased market share • Competitors are weak • Competitors do not respond to new strategies	**New strategies from competitors** • Price wars • Slow or no reaction to new strategies • New technology

Twenty Five Questions
Are you ready to answer the angel's questions?

These top 25 questions are what most angels will ask your team about your business. You can also include this template as an initial summary for angels, bankers or investors. You should have the answers to these questions readily available when seeking angels for your new venture.

1. What type of business do you have?
2. What is the purpose of this business?
3. What is the key message or phrase to describe your business in one sentence?
4. What is your reason for starting or expanding your business?
5. What is your product or service?
6. Can you list three unique benefits of your product?
7. Do you have data sheets, brochures, diagrams, sketches, photographs, related press releases or other documentation about your product/service?
8. What is the product application?
9. What led you to develop your product?
10. Is this product or service used in connection with other products?
11. List the top three objections to buying your product/service immediately?
12. When will your product be available?
13. Who is your target customer?
14. Who is your competition?
15. How is your product differentiated from that of your competition?
16. What is the pricing of your product versus your competition?
17. Are you making any special offers?
18. What plans do you have for advertising and promotions?
19. How will you finance company growth?
20. Do you have the management team needed to achieve your goals?
21. Do you have or intend to have a shareholders' agreement?
22. What are your investment requirements and offering details?
23. What have you personally invested to date?
24. Tell me about your team?
25. What is your exit strategy?

11

Understanding Financial Statements

Introduction

Every business decision is in some way related to a business's finance. We consider the return on any expenditure and we review our available cash before we decide to spend. Every business develops financial statements, but surprising most people can't really read what they mean. Many say they can read the profit and loss account but often when they say that they really mean they can read the bottom line that points to a profit or a loss. They don't understand how financial statements can be manipulated and how, all too often, they do not represent the real value of the business.

If an experienced person examines a set of financial statements, they can tell you so much about a business and its problem areas. Most business owners don't get to use this information because they don't truly understand financial statements.

The purpose of this chapter is to help you see why you must understand financial information and how you can use it effectively to manage or assess a business. It is important that business owners and managers take ownership of the financial management of the company and not give it to an outside person (such as their accountant) as assumptions will be made that can change the value of a business significantly. Informed people take the time to understand the intricacies of financial statements and don't rely 100 percent on accountants advice.

To summarize, the objectives of this chapter are to:

- Understand financial terminology and use this to accurately read financial statements
- Empower you to be in control of financial statements and ensure they are accurate
- Understand how financial statements can be manipulated.

This chapter must start at the beginning with the accounting terminology. Please read on and the subject will become clearer. You will then see the importance of understanding finances.

Understanding financial statements

The main components of financial statements are:

- Statement of financial performance (more commonly known as the Profit and Loss Statement)
- Statement of financial position (or commonly known as the Balance Sheet)

The **Statement of financial performance** (or profit and loss statement) shows a business's income less expenses over a period of time. Note that it is over a period of time. That means results are artificially distorted because of the time period imposed. For example, if a company spends an enormous amount on marketing activities in one period, but the sales from those activities are in the next period, the bottom line does not reflect accurately the matching of income and expenses. In comparing periods, management needs to take note of this artificial barrier when reviewing financial statements. There are other distortions that can occur, and these are explained in a later section.

If revenue is greater than expenses, there is a profit for the period.

If revenue is less than expenses, there is a loss for the period.

The **Statement of financial position** (or balance sheet) is a summary of the assets, liabilities and the amount invested by the business owners in a business at a particular time.

There are three main components of a balance sheet

- Assets
- Liabilities
- Shareholders equity or proprietors' funds

Assets are something of value owned where the benefit is received over time. Assets can be

- Current – where the benefit is realized within one year
- Non-current – where the benefit is realized in more than one year

What may be surprising is assets can be recorded differently for different businesses and the assumptions adopted determine the asset value in the balance sheet. For example, assume we are in a boom property time and a business revalues the property it owns. The asset of the property may be shown at $2 million in the balance sheet. Then the market has a downturn and it may be worth only $1.5 million. How should the company show the value of that property? More importantly did the directors show that devaluation or not?

There are certain rules in place for revaluing assets and showing their valuation. Directors must explain the way they value the property but for an amateur reader of financial statements it would be very easy to miss the potential devaluation of the property if the company doesn't recognize it.

This is similarly the case with other assets which may be shown at cost price and be worth far more than the cost price; or for that matter be worth far less than the cost price.

Some examples of different types of assets are:

- Cash at Bank
- Inventory - which may be shown at cost, replacement value or market selling value. The valuation method adopted can have a major impact on the financial results.
- Accounts receivable - which may or may not allow for a reduction due to bad and doubtful debts
- Property, plant and equipment – may be shown at cost or other values. Often companies write off the full cost of smaller items of plant and equipment and unknowingly can devalue their business by doing this. This is explained further in a later section
- Intellectual property – may be included as an asset or may be expensed and therefore form a part of the balance sheet.

Liabilities are amounts owed by a business. They are shown at the liability value at the date of the balance sheet.

- Current liabilities are payable within one year.
- Non-current liabilities payable in more than one year.

Some examples of different types of liabilities are

- Bank overdraft or loans
- Trade creditors
- Other creditors
- Hire purchase agreements
- Loans from shareholders
- Contingent liabilities
- Future commitments

There are some issues with accurately reflecting liabilities, especially contingent liabilities, which may be only detailed in the notes to the accounts and often not read.

Shareholders equity or proprietor's funds represent the money invested in a business by the owners and in a company it includes:

- The amount paid for shares

- Accumulated profits of the company less any losses to date and dividends paid
- Other reserves of the business

In the balance sheet, assets less liabilities equals the equity of the business.

Why financial statements are prepared

Many think that if 20 accountants were provided the same information on a business, they will all come up with the same financial statements for a business. This is not necessarily the case.

To understand why the financial statements may be different, let's first consider why the statements are being prepared. A business may need to prepare statements to:

- Satisfy taxation requirements – lodge BAS and annual taxation returns
- Satisfy corporations law as companies are required to prepare annual financial statements
- For management purposes
- For financiers
- For investors
- To value the business for sale

Conflicting agendas?

Reviewing the list above raises a number of conflicting agendas. For example, when preparing financial statements for taxation purposes you want to minimize tax. If preparing financial statements for a sale or to raise equity, the business wants to show the highest potential profit. In summary, the following list illustrates the potential conflicting agendas when preparing the financial statements:

- Minimize tax
- Show the best profit shown for financiers
- Meet performance requirements by management
- Obtain the best price for business
- Politics and remuneration (e.g. management bonus if certain results are met)

How can financial statements be manipulated or distorted?

When reviewing a set of statements it is important to realize that the information could in some way be distorted. This happens because there are various rules that accountants need to adopt when preparing financial statements, however, most of them have a degree of flexibility within these rules. With a property valuation, a piece of land could be valued at current market value, prior market value or fire sale value if it needs to be sold very quickly. Other assets or even income and expenses can be shown in a variety of ways. The owner of a business, an investor or a person reading the financial statements MUST be concerned with the way the figures in the financial statements are shown. There is a clear need to understand the assumptions adopted in the preparation of the financial statements.

Note that the directors of every company are ultimately responsible for how the financial results are shown in the financial statements. Whilst the accountant should have input, it is not appropriate to leave all decisions to them; management should take responsibility to ensure the financial statements represent a true and fair view of the company's results.

Some common ways financial statements are manipulated or distorted include:

- Assets can be shown at cost or at other valuations – unrealized gains and losses may or may not be recognized
- Taxation treatment influences accounting treatment and if a business brings in all of tax deductions as expenses (rather than just claiming the deduction in the income tax return) it can reduce strength of the balance sheet and therefore the company's value
- Trying to minimize tax payable. This can be accomplished by not recognizing income into one period or by bringing in the next periods expenses
- Various assumptions can be adopted. For example, how and when income is recognized on long term contracts or how the depreciation rate is used to write off assets.
- Using an artificial barrier in the preparation of the profit and loss statement for a period
- Setting the balance sheet is at a particular time before or after asset disposal or accumulation

How can a profit and loss statement be distorted?

Income

- Revenue is only recognized when received as opposed to when invoiced
- Use of incorrect cut off date for sales – e.g. invoices are not processed until the next month so they are left out
- Income is included from the next period - e.g. there is a deposit on a sale in one period but the work to complete the job is not undertaken until the next period. Some people may recognize the deposit or in fact the total sale when the deposit is received
- Closing stock can be changed dramatically depending on which valuation method is adopted which can have dramatic effects on the gross profit

- Expenses are incurred in one period but the income is included in the next period (e.g. export market development expenditure)
- Some businesses may work on cash or an accruals basis.

Expenses

- Expenses may be understated to make profit look higher, or
- Overstated to reduce profit
- Different assumptions can alter the amount of an expense - e.g. depreciation rates applied may write the asset off over three years when the equipment will last and benefits will be derived over 10 years.
- Some businesses may work on cash or an accruals basis.

How assets can be manipulated

Some assets are shown at a "value" that is determined by circumstances. This "value" could be based on cost price, current value or independent valuation.

Cost of goods sold

If a business sells stock, it is important to understand how the cost of goods sold is calculated, and it should be accurately recorded.

Cost of goods sold is calculated as the opening stock value at the beginning of period, plus purchases made during the period and less the closing stock at end of period.

This figure is then deducted from sales to calculate gross profit.

The effect of applying a different value to the closing stock of a business can be achieved by changing the method of valuation or by not accurately calculating the stock. An example follows:

On the left side, in the following table, the value of the closing stock is $25,000 but to the right, the value of the closing stock is $5,000. Management may justify such a difference in many ways. By changing the value of the closing stock, management can increase or decrease gross profit very easily, in the case of this example, by $20,000.

Effect of closing stock

Sales	100,000	Sales	100,000
Opening stock	10,000	Opening stock	10,000
Add purchases	30,000	Add purchases	30,000
Less closing stock	25,000	Less closing stock	5,000
Total cost	(15,000)	Total cost	(35,000)
Gross profit	85,000	Gross profit	65,000

Is a balance sheet accurate?

There are many common mistakes in the way the financial statements of a business are shown which can have an effect when being reviewed. These include:

- Assets or liabilities are often not split correctly between current and non-current categories
- Some treat all shareholders' or directors' loans as current liabilities when they may be non-current liabilities
- The financial statements may include the total lease or hire purchase liability as either current or non-current liabilities
- Sometimes assets are written off rather than depreciated over their useful life
- Sales invoices with deposits may be treated as income when deposits are received – without allowing for the costs to produce sales items
- Creditors may be understated
- Many businesses ignore work in progress and do not recognize it as an asset

Notes to the financial statements

The financial statements also include "Notes to the financial statements" which are a summary of the major accounting policies adopted. They also provide additional information to assist in the interpretation of the report. The irony is that despite them often numbering twenty pages or more for a public company, most people do not read them. If the notes are not read and understood it is difficult to understand the results presented by the directors and to pick up any distortions that may exist. Although laborious, understanding a financial statement can provide huge advantage in assessing a company's performance or valuation.

Directors' duties

The directors of a company are subject to certain requirements which include

- They have a duty to ensure financial statements are prepared that represent a true and fair view of the financial position of the company
- They must comply with all accounting standards and laws when preparing those financial statements
- They must ensure the company is able to pay its debts as and when they become due. i.e. they must remain solvent. See Chapter 15.

Based on the foregoing it is therefore essential that financial statements are an accurate reflection of the position of the company. Directors shouldn't be too conservative and undervalue the assets of the company, nor should they be too optimistic and inflate the company's position. If the directors of the company partake in "creative accounting" there are serious consequences. Recent high profile cases where directors have been sent to jail highlight this.

As the financial statements are one of the main reports provided to external parties, it is imperative that directors "take ownership" of the presentation of the information.

Financial statements versus income tax return

When reviewing a set of financial statements for a public company, there is normally a detailed note explaining the taxation due by the company. This results from the differences that exist in the Corporations Law and Accounting Standards that states how a company's financial statements should be prepared, versus the taxation laws that state what is taxable income, and what are allowable deductions. Using a simple example, we know that in business many major decisions can be made over a lunch meeting and we accept this is a business expense. However under taxation laws, this may or may not be tax deductible and it may or may not be subject to fringe benefits tax, depending on the policies adopted by the company. The question then arises how does a business account for differences between financial statements and income tax returns?

In many smaller companies, the accountant will allow for any tax deductible items (such as 100% write off of smaller items of plant and equipment) in the financial statements. The better alternative is that the accountant should ensure the financial statements represent a true and fair view of the results of the company, and then bring in the most deductions in the income tax return. A company income tax return actually includes two columns where the first is a summary of the trading results of the company (per the profit and loss statements) and the second column allows adjustments to be included to ensure you pay the correct tax. This means a business can still claim a tax deduction for 100% of the cost of smaller assets if the business is eligible, BUT the true profit or loss in your financial statements is shown.

It may be easier for the accountant to just claim 100% of everything in your financial statements with no adjustments in your income tax return, but if the directors allow this and they happen to be considering selling the business, they can significantly devalue the business. Most businesses are sold at a multiple of the profit, where a Price to Earnings (PE) ratio is applied. The following is a simple example to explain this point:

Assume a company is sold that has a profit before tax of $100,000.

The trading results are:

Income	$500,000
Less expenses	$400,000
Net profit before tax	$100,000

Now assume the owner could sell the business at a value equal to a PE ratio of four. The sale price would therefore be $400,000.

If however, there were considerable tax deductions included in the financial statements that may only have needed to be included in the tax return the result could have been different.

Let's assume there was $15,000 of smaller items of plant and equipment that would have lasted 10 years, but instead the accountant just wrote off the entire cost in the year of acquisition. *Assume those items of plant and equipment were bought at the end of the financial year so depreciation on them would be minimal in that financial year and for the purposes of this calculation, we will ignore it.*

The results may be as follows:

Income	$500,000
Less expenses	$385,000
Net profit before tax	$115,000

The company would still pay income tax on $100,000 as the accountant could claim the $15,000 as a tax deduction in the tax return, but for accounting purposes, the financial statements show a $15,000 higher profit.

Assume the owner of the business on the sale could still obtain a PE ratio of four; the sale price would therefore be $460,000 – a gain of $60,000 just by correctly accounting for the plant and equipment.

When this is raised with accountants, they generally state that "*an adjustment can be made when we sell the business and we can simply change entries in the valuation*". The argument that it's easier to just do it properly in the first place is valid. Those who have sold a business in the past, know how hard it is to start changing the "profit" shown in the financial statements. You have to argue for every change that increases the price. Why not do it right in the first place and save yourself the argument.

Are your financial statements accurate?

The challenge for all business owners is to review your financial statements, or for those that are looking at investing in a business to review the statements presented and consider whether they accurately reflect the business.

What changes do you make to your statements to make them more accurate?

Key revenue and expense drivers of business

Most businesses have approximately five revenue items and five expense items that make a difference to the business. These items are known as "key drivers" of the business. Changes in these "key drivers" really make a difference to how the business is performing. Unfortunately most profit and loss statements do not adequately highlight the key drivers of the business and instead they are hidden amongst the myriad of other often immaterial items.

For example, one set of financial statements for a business with in excess of $1 million in turnover revealed an all too common occurrence. It showed "Sales" with 99% of revenue included and then some immaterial other revenue items including interest and sundries. There is no way that the owner of that business could review the income in the financial statements and make any meaningful plans.

It would have been preferable had they split the sales between product A, product B and product C. Alternatively should the income be split between region A, region B and region C or wholesale, retail and direct sales? If done well, when the statements are reviewed management can easily see which products or regions were performing and what sales areas needed more attention.

The problem is that most accountants, not all, have little interest in this aspect of your business.

With the advent of MYOB and similar bookkeeping programs that detail many different expense items, people regularly have between 20 and 40 expense items. In reviewing the expenses of many profit and loss statements you can see expenses detailed that may only have a small amount of expenditure, yet they are still recorded. In the case of the company mentioned above with turnover of more than $1 million, there were about 50 expense items and some with less than $100 included. Yet the key expenditure items showed only a total amount and therefore provided management with very little information. These items were lost within two pages of immaterial expenses.

The need to consider what you need to know to effectively manage your business is important. Designing the financial statements to ensure you could easily extract that information is an important step in setting up your company books. Unfortunately, most people leave the design of their financial statements to a bookkeeper who most likely has no experience or very limited experience in managing a business.

It is suggested that you review a business's financial statements to see if they accurately reflect your key drivers of the business. If not then speak to the person preparing the statements and ask that the statements are changed to reflect what is needed to effectively manage the business. Please note that there are very few laws that state what income and expense items you need to include in your financial statements. It is up to management to ensure the financial statements are meaningful and can be effectively used for management purposes. A less detailed list of expenses in the profit and loss can prove far easier to read and can be more meaningful.

Make sure you have an effective profit and loss statement to assist you in effectively managing the business.

Summary

Every part of a business is either affected by or affects the financial results of the company. We know that despite there being a world of information available in financial statements many people do not accurately read what is presented or cannot access this information. Worst still, many people manipulate the financial statements of a business and this manipulation often goes undetected.

This chapter has provided information to assist you to better understand the financial results of a business – whether as an investor or as part of a management team growing a business. Too often people do not really understand their business's financial results and this means that management cannot perform at their optimum level.

Anyone using financial statements should be able to read them properly and that is why we have highlighted the components of financial statements and the numerous ways the financial results can be deliberately or unintentionally distorted. It is a director's duty to ensure this does not happen.

It is important that management ensure the information presented in their financial statements can be used effectively to manage the business. If you do this and present the statements with information on the key drivers of the business, it will allow you to make decisions far more effectively. Your attention will be directed where it matters – to approximately the five main income areas of the business and the five major expense areas of the business. Most other income or expense items are immaterial.

12

Understanding Sales & Marketing

Introduction

This brief chapter is provided as a simple introduction for entrepreneurs and mentors to better understand the basics of marketing and sales. Marketing and sales are distinctly different functions within an organization. They need to be looked at separately.

What is marketing?

Marketing is a strategic function. It defines customer behavior in regard to your product or service. Five key questions define what marketing is all about:

- What are we selling and what do they buy?
- Who are we selling too?
- How are we going to sell and how do they buy?
- Why are people going to purchase this product from us?
- Where do we sell and where do they buy?

How you answer the above questions determines the basics of your marketing plan.

A simple example of the need for a clear marketing plan is the development of the "Product Positioning Statement" which generally takes the form as follows:

> For **[TARGET MARKET]**, **[PRODUCT]** is, among **[PRODUCT CATEGORY]**, **[SINGLE MOST IMPORTANT CLAIM]**, because **[SINGLE MOST IMPORTANT SUPPORT STATEMENT]**.

Let's look at a simple example, a fictitious automobile manufacturer, Fokswagen, with a typical family people mover.

> For **large families on the move**, **the Fokswagen** is, among **people movers**, **the most spacious and luxurious**, because **we care about your family's real needs**.

The evolution from station wagons to people movers took innovative thinking along with careful market research. Without market research the revolutionary progress of people movers would have been slower.

Thorough market research will allow ventures to more easily reach their goals. Good marketing develops qualified customer leads.

What is sales?

Whether you are selling a cold drink at a football game or a complex service or product, the following five steps are always involved in the sales process:

Step 1: Is the customer aware of your offering?

Step 2: Does the customer understand what you are offering?

Step 3: Does the customer believe that you can deliver the product, service and the benefits?

Step 4: Does the customer believe you are the best source compared to other alternatives (including not purchasing)?

Step 5: Is the customer committed to purchasing?

Sales is a chosen tactic of the marketing process. You can choose to sell online. You can choose to hire an outbound sales force or a telemarketing team. In its simplest form, the sales process converts a lead into a closed sale.

Any company that is proceeding down the path of selling a product must have people, processes and tools. The single most important item is people. If you do not have effective sales people, then clearly, you will not sell effectively. Who are your sales people and who manages your sales staff are key questions for any company and will drive success.

How important is the sales team?

If you have to ask, you have some work to do before you meet with prospective investors.

Within a typical sales force it is often said that 20 percent of the staff bring in 50 to 80 percent of the business. For an entrepreneur who manages to hire (or is) a single salesman who can only deliver mediocre performance, prospects for success are greatly diminished. As much as we would like to believe it, great products rarely sell themselves.

Processes

- What is the sales plan?
- Are people held accountable to the sales plan?
- Generating leads. Are your leads exceptional? Too many companies chase leads that are not.
- Are your sales people motivated? Compensation and incentive plans are processes that make the engine tick over.

Required sales tools

- Sales play book – This documents sales questions, objections and the closing process for your products
- Feature and benefit list
- Sales materials
- Sales automation system

Tips

- Be prepared
- Focus on benefits not features
- Listen to the customer, don't talk too much
- Ask just a few good questions
- Know how to handle objections
- Ask for the order (Note that just over 50 percent of all professional sales people actually ask for the order - hard to believe)

... with our ethanol/diesel injection technology, which we've defined belongs in the US market initially, the real customers for our products are truck fleet owners. To secure our market we need to secure the interest of truck and truck component manufacturers who will drive the process. To get the manufacturers excited you must get their customers excited, which are the fleets, which is why we are focusing on getting UPS, US Army & Wal-Mart fleets committed to trialing our technology. I'm regularly surprised at how many inventors do not understand the difference between stakeholders and customers."

Greg Beaver,
Investor and entrepreneur

Understanding the product adoption lifecycle

When a product has not entered the market before, additional barriers will exist. In this case, the product adoption lifecycle needs to be well understood.

In the diagram below, you will notice that customers may take a differing approach to purchasing depending on their risk tolerance.

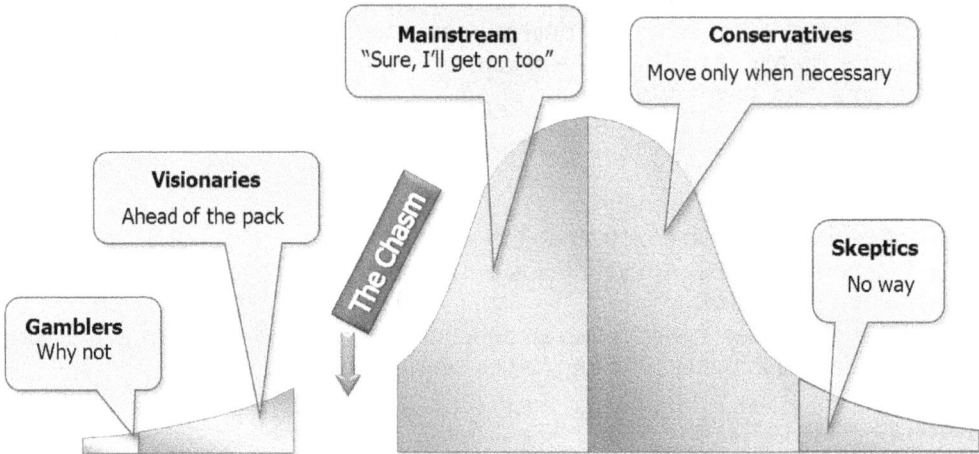

Product Adoption Lifecycle

It is dealing with the chasm where a company can lose momentum. The chasm can develop for many reasons. It is possible that early adopters are already tapped and the mainstream has not seen sufficient evidence to get involved (yet). It's also possible that the entrepreneur or the sales team simply becomes bored or frustrated with the process and/or cannot manage the increased sales and sales support. Managing this process does have a big effect on success of a venture.

This chapter is intended to provide some stimulation for people to seek further knowledge on marketing and sales. There are many books that delve into the topics above and we encourage you read them, or better yet, to surround yourselves with people with an intimate and proven knowledge of sales and marketing. Without the knowledge of good sales and marketing a great product will get nowhere quickly.

13

Corporate Governance

Corporate governance is the set of processes, policies, and agreements which affect the way in which a corporation is directed, administered or controlled. Corporate governance includes the relationships of the many players involved (the stakeholders) and the goals for which the corporation is governed. The principal players are the shareholders, management and the board of directors. Stakeholders also include employees, suppliers, customers, banks and other lenders, regulators, the environment and the community at large.

What you need to know about corporate governance

Corporate governance can be an expensive distraction but it does need to be understood, after all, every successful company will eventually need to develop workable corporate governance guidelines at some point.

For early-stage ventures the company will want to define processes that include the following:

1. Is the board of directors correctly established, operating effectively and meeting regularly?
2. Is the company operating solvently (can it pay all its bills)?
3. Are the shareholders being represented fairly?
4. Are employees, vendors and customers cared for adequately?
5. Is the CEO remuneration defined by and understood by the board?
6. Does the company operate ethically and responsibly in all areas?
7. Do board members have full and direct access to information relating to customers, employment and finance? (are financial records, bank statements, etc., provided to all on request)

If a company cannot answer any of the above with confidence, then it needs to address these issues immediately. As a young company, it is possible that the processes and/or documentation may not exist for some of the above items, however, the thinking must include checks on any issues that will affect fairness to all involved.

The value of good corporate governance

Good corporate governance will be noticed by all involved in a company. The company will develop more reliable employees, investors, management, vendors and customers. It's basically a way to state clearly "we operate honestly and with integrity". Done well, it can create the following:
1. Less stress on the board of directors
2. Less concerns from shareholders
3. More reliable and dedicated staff
4. Vendors who are more readily willing to support the company's efforts

Developing good corporate governance

One of the best first steps to develop good corporate governance it to bring in a well versed company chairman who can run board meetings effectively. A good chairman will drive company board meetings efficiently and effectively. They will separate management issues from board issues. In a small company it is common for management issues to be bought up at board meetings. A good chairman will set any management issues aside (unless very relevant) until the board meeting is closed and then open the management meeting to allow the information to be provided.

When you find the words "If I may speak, mister chairman?" commonly used in a board meeting it is a good sign that the chairman is driving the meeting correctly. Often the chairman is an investor or an independent wishing to assist the company. For small companies, board fees are provided in the form of share or option issues.

14

Contingency and Solvency

A weakness in many young companies is the lack of good cash-flow analysis. Detailed cash-flow reporting provides board members with confidence as to solvency issues and can serve to motivate the company to address issues before they appear rather than later. The contingency account and solvency report serve to address careful measurement of a company's current position from within management.

The contingency account

Discipline is required when addressing contingency funds. Contingency should be deposited into a separate savings account to satisfy three to six months of cash requirements. Typically, with a poorly managed company, contingencies are spent on "essential" and often unbudgeted items rather than being truly reserved for the ongoing cash requirements of the existing business.

"It's OK, because we will close that big deal tomorrow and we can repay the contingency. If we don't run this additional advertising we won't meet our forecasts."

The problem with this is that when (usually not if) tomorrow's sale does not appear, then part or all contingency goes up in smoke.

Investors want to know that their investment has a contingency in hand when problems occur. Most don't like to be asked to provide additional capital and many won't.

Solvency reporting

The solvency report is simple and essential. It provides knowledge of where the company is now including allowances for accruals such as taxes, vacation pay and insurance. It answers the question "If we shut the company down today, what would be the cash position".

Unlike the accounting reports it seeks to address the following:
1. It's unlikely that we would get anything for our intellectual property. (Assumes $0 value)
2. It takes a conservative approach to accounts receivable. (e.g. assumes 80 percent are recoverable within 60 days)
3. It discounts any paid up insurance.
4. It takes into account federal, state and payroll taxes owing.
5. It allows for accrued vacation pay and long service leave.
6. It assumes that assets that may be difficult to convert to cash have a low or $0 value.

A simple example can be seen in the following table:

Solvency Report as at 14 August 2008

Current Assets		Current Liabilities	
Chequing Account	$120,000	Accounts Payable	$34,567
Savings Account	$ 60,000	Payroll Liabilities	$12,000
Inventory	$ 7,600	Taxes	$ 4,500
		Short term loan	$ -
		GST	$ 1,450
	$187,600		$52,517

Surplus Assets	$135,083

In the above example, once a director knows that the report is accurate and has checked the basis for the derivation with regard to solvency, they can be confident that they are satisfying their governance requirements. In this case, a net position of $135,000 is understood and therefore the company is solvent.

The days of "We think we can make payroll next week" are nearly numbered. Directors are personally responsible and it now takes a brave (or wealthy) director to be involved in a company bordering on insolvency. Most sophisticated investors will not take such a risks.

15

Measuring Investment Maturity and Potential for Success

Introduction

Accessing the maturity of an investment opportunity and its potential for success generates valuable knowledge to all involved in a venture including the entrepreneur, mentor and the investor.

Angels Institute members use a tool which develops the Angels Institute Maturity Indicator (AIMI) that can assist in determining where the maturity of a company lies on a scale of one to 10.

Used collaboratively, it is also a valuable tool to uncover problem areas within an opportunity. Once identified, these problem areas may create real issues or may offer solutions that can easily be addressed.

Angels Institute Investment Maturity Indicator (AIMI)

The assessment uses the form displayed at the end of the chapter. After a review of the company, participants are requested to provide a score on a scale of one to 10 for each of 10 business elements.

The elements examined are as follows:
1. Leadership
2. Business team
3. Controls & process
4. Investor returns
5. Unfair advantage
6. Alliance partners
7. Distribution
8. Market size
9. Finances
10. Customer need

If the venture is still at the ideas stage then an AIMI of two to five will be the expectation. Likewise, a more mature venture, that has developed first sales and a cash flow from revenues, will more than likely develop an AIMI of between five and 10. The flexibility of the system also allows for a basic concept to be able to generate reasonable scores where the business team is strong and capable and have done their homework.

Angels Institute Success Maturity Indicator (AISI)

The Angels Institute Success Indicator (AISI), may also be determined as part of this process. Participants are asked to indicate with a value of between 0 percent and 100 percent the expected level of success by the company for each of the 10 business elements. The AISI provides participants with a measure the potential success for the venture.

If we had a crystal ball it might be easier. Tools like the AIMI and AISI can be valuable in assessing a company. They are subjective tools and are only as good as the people using them. They do, however, go a long way to methodically uncover known and unknown quantities of an early-stage investment opportunity.

Angels Institute Maturity Indicator (AIMI)
and Angels Institute Success Indicator (AISI)

Company Name: _____
Date: _____

Team Name: _____
Event: _____

Determines the stage of maturity of any business investment opportunity and, in turn, targets areas of potential improvement.

© Angels Institute 2009. All rights reserved. Printed with permission.

Indicator:	1	2	3	4	5	6	7	8	9	10	Scores /10	Success Odds %	Example of a perfect 10
	Start-up			Early-Stage				Established					
	Vision/Idea	Documents Prototypes		Customer Proof		Revenues		Established historical sales					
	Learning			Delivering				Exceptional					
Leadership — Is the leader the very best person?											/10	%	If we offered $1m per year would we get better?
Business Team — Is the business team the very best?											/10	%	Is every vacancy filled by the best?
Controls & Process — Is every aspect under control?											/10	%	Business processes, inventory, HR, sales, etc.
Investor Returns — Is the investor securing 35% pa											/10	%	35% actual cash return would score a 10
Unfair Advantage — Does the company beat their competitors 100% of the time?											/10	%	Monopoly
Alliance Partners — Are alliance partners covering 50% of marketing costs?											/10	%	Alliance is stable and of proven high value
Distribution — Distribution channel established											/10	%	Distribution channel established and operating in a mature manner
Market Size — Very large and growing market											/10	%	Every customer will consider purchasing within 12 months
Finances — Fully funded											/10	%	Angel fully committed to support the future
Customer Need — Customer need is great and satisfied by product or service											/10	%	Customer has too much pain without solution
Indicator:	1	2	3	4	5	6	7	8	9	10	AIMI	AISI	AIMI is the sum of Scores/10 and AISI is the average of Success Odds

Low scores will result in many areas and do not reflect on the entrepreneur but rather the current early stage position of the company. Some will reflect that some aspects simply have not been dealt with because of the stage of the venture. All scores reflect the current maturity of the venture in each catecgory. Note that a $1m salary may buy a quality person and entry to an industry at a high level but may not provide the passion of the entrepreneur. Should the entrepreneur be positioned as head of R & D?

16

The Shareholders' Agreement

Introduction

Issues involving shareholders' agreements can be complex; especially when you realize that no one knows the true outcome of an early-stage venture.

A shareholders' agreement is not about trust or hostile positioning. The premise that the shareholders' agreement represents all shareholders equally should be a good starting point in all discussions. The shareholders' agreement should develop good communication and a common understanding of the path forward. It should assist in developing a strong relationship to all shareholders involved with the venture.

By going through the development of a shareholders' agreement, those involved are forced to discuss and think about potential major issues that may appear in the future. Doing so now will prevent potential upset and expensive legal bills in the future. It should cement a stronger relationship between all shareholders.

All investors would prefer to have a shareholders' agreement in place to protect their interests as minority owners. Such agreements protect shareholders from the biased opinions of majority owner(s). Majority owner(s) often see constraints that protect the minority shareholders as being too restrictive.

... investors cannot afford to invest in a company that becomes a family business. Such an investment simply will not provide a means to cash in on any gain. Exit strategies must be realisable.

You can't count on a majority owner always being the person that shareholders will have to work with. For example, the majority owner may pass away and shareholders may find themselves dealing with that shareholders' spouse. A clear record of what shareholders agreed to, allows others to understand and implement the agreement if they come in later in the process.

The best shareholders' agreements are stored away and never used. Provided the shareholders agree, content can be changed as the company progresses.

In this chapter we look at the contents of a shareholders' agreement and at what is appropriate for each stage of the company's development.

Components of a shareholders' agreement

Let's take a look at the various components of a full shareholders' agreement to learn a little more about their function.

General introduction

This simply spells out the obvious including the fact that the shareholders are the owners of all of the issued shares of the company and that the shareholders and the company wish to further the interests of the company by establishing rules that govern the management and operation of the company.

Right of first refusal

This section constrains any shareholder from selling shares without notification and without first offering the shares for sale to the existing shareholders. The shareholders' agreement may authorize some transfers that restructure a shareholder's holding, without changing the underlying ownership.

The section contains clauses spelling out the notice required and what happens if the existing shareholders don't wish to purchase the other shareholder's shares.

The purpose is to ensure that any future transactions occur with full knowledge of all parties and that original shareholders have an opportunity to secure a larger equity position in the company if they so desire before an outside party may participate. The rationale for these types of provisions is that the shareholders have agreed to enter a business undertaking between themselves, and a third party should not be able to acquire an interest in the business without the approval of existing shareholders or without those shareholders first having the opportunity to acquire the interest available for sale.

A relatively simple example below provides an indication of content.

> Except as otherwise noted in this agreement, no Shareholder shall sell or otherwise transfer or dispose of any Shares unless the following conditions have been complied with:
>
>> (a) The transferring Shareholder shall give the Company and each other Shareholder (Recipient Shareholder) written notice (Transfer Notice) of the terms, (including the price per share, number of shares to be transferred (Transfer Shares) and the name of the proposed transferee) on which he proposes to transfer his shares.
>>
>> (b) Within thirty days after receipt of a Transfer Notice (Offer Period) each Recipient Shareholder may make an offer to purchase some or all of the Transfer Shares on the terms of the Transfer Notice by giving the Company notice in writing (Acceptance Notice).
>>
>> (c) The Company will, within two (2) Business Days of the end of the Offer Period, give a notice (Allocation Notice) to each Recipient Shareholder who has given the Company an Acceptance Notice (Accepting Shareholder) allocating the Transfer Shares as follows:
>>
>> (i) if offers for Transfer Shares are equal to the number of Transfer Shares, the Company must allocate the number of

Transfer Shares requested by each Accepting Shareholder in the Acceptance Notices; and

(ii)   if offers for Transfer Shares are more than the number of Transfer Shares, the Company must allocate:

    (A)   to each Accepting Shareholder the lesser of that Shareholder's Relevant Proportion (i.e. the proportion that the Shares held by the Accepting Shareholder bears to the Shares held by all of the Accepting Shareholders) of Transfer Shares and the number of Transfer Shares requested; and

    (B)   the remaining Transfer Shares to each Accepting Shareholder that has unfilled offers on a pro rata basis according to their unfilled offers.

An Allocation Notice constitutes an acceptance to sell the Transfer Shares identified in the Allocation Notice to the Shareholder specified in the Allocation Notice.

(d)   Completion of the transfer of Transfer Shares must take place within 30 days of the date of the Allocation Notice.

(e)   If all the Shares which the transferring Shareholder proposes to sell are not purchased by the other Shareholders, in accordance with subparagraph (c) above, the transferring Shareholder may make a bona fide transfer of all of the Transfer Shares to the prospective purchaser named, and upon the other terms stated, in his notice of proposed sale. If the transferring Shareholder shall fail to make such sale within ninety days following the expiration of the time provided in subparagraph (c) above for the exercise of the right to purchase by other Shareholders, the right of the transferring Shareholder to make the proposed sale shall terminate.

Restriction on transfer by gift or pledge

This is designed to prevent shares from being transferred to others through gift or pledge (i.e. given as security). Typically, the shareholders agreement will provide that the board of directors or shareholders may approve such a transaction.

Purchase of Shares (Death or Incompetency)

This provides the ability for the other shareholders to enter into an agreement to purchase the shares held by a deceased shareholder. This may be accomplished through a key-man life insurance policy in the case of the entrepreneur and/or in some cases may be purchased through a promissory note over time.

Additional shareholders

The shareholders' agreement should provide that a person may not become a shareholder of the company (by the issue of shares or the transfer of shares) unless that person has first agreed to be bound by the shareholders' agreement. This is often done by a document called a Deed of Accession or New Shareholders' Deed. The following is an example:

The Board may only allot or issue any New Capital to a person that is not a Shareholder if the person has executed, and delivered to the Company, a New Shareholder Deed. (Issue of new shares)

The Company must refuse to register the transfer of any Security unless the transferee has entered into a New Shareholder Deed (unless the transferee is already a Shareholder), and that transfer is permitted by this document. (Transfer of shares)

Election of directors

This clause ensures that minority investors maintain a say in the operation of the business. It typically sets out the composition of the board and the manner of appointment of directors. It is common for an investor to seek a right to appoint a director to the board of the company. The shareholders' agreement may provide that the investor will only have this right while the investor holds a minimum proportion of the company's shares. It is designed specifically to address the potential for the following:

- An entrepreneur may or may not be the best choice of CEO for the business.
- An entrepreneur may desire to maintain the company in the current state of operation when the original intention was to generate an exit. It is not uncommon for an entrepreneur to secure a good salary and be satisfied while the company no longer progresses toward the most favorable outcome.
- A majority shareholder may have a conflict of interest that is maintained to the detriment of minority shareholders.

In the above cases the board has been structured to force a reasonable direction by the board as defined. This can become quite complex. A relatively simple example below provides an indication of content.

The board of directors will comprise:

(a)   two Directors appointed by the Founding Shareholders; and

(b)   one Director appointed by the Investor.

A shareholder who is entitled to appoint a Director may remove that Director and appoint another Director in that Director's place.

Each shareholder must exercise its rights as a holder of Shares to ensure that the composition of the board of directors is as set out above.

Tag along rights (piggyback rights)

In order that each shareholder is treated equally, there exists the possibility that a potential buyer can offer one or more shareholders a large purchase opportunity that is attractive and that other shareholders may not be able to otherwise participate in. The Right of Cooperative Sale ensures that all shareholders are able to participate in a partial exit. For example:

> If a Shareholder (Seller) proposes to sell any of the Seller's Shares to a third party, the Seller must first give each other Shareholder (Offerees) notice (Sale Notice) of the proposed sale specifying:
>
> > (a)   the proposed buyer;
> >
> > (b)   the number of Shares that the Seller proposes to sell (Sale Shares);
> >
> > (c)   the price per Share at which the Seller proposes to sell the Shares (Sale Price);
> >
> > (d)   the proposed settlement date; and
> >
> > (e)   any other relevant terms and conditions of the proposed sale.
>
> Each Offeree may within 10 Business Days after receiving a Sale Notice give notice (Tag Along Notice) to the Seller of its wish to sell on the terms in the Sale Notice a percentage of its total holding of Shares equal to the percentage of the Seller's total holding of Shares that the Sale Shares represent.
>
> If an Offeree or Offerees serves or serve a Tag Along Notice on the Seller, the Seller may only sell the Sale Shares, if at the same time as the sale of the Sale Shares, all Shares specified in the Tag Along Notice (Tag Along Securities) are sold at the Sale Price per security and on the same terms as the Sale Shares are sold.

Drag along rights

In the event of a reasonable offer that requires a 50 percent or more of the company to be sold, it is frustrating when one finds shareholders not willing to allow the transaction to occur. This clause allows the simple majority of shareholders to force other shareholders to participate to allow the transaction to occur. For example,

> 1   Drag along
>
> 1.1   Third party offer
>
> > If the Company or a Shareholder receives an offer from a bona fide buyer of all the Shares in the Company (Offeror), it must give each other party notice, on behalf of the Offeror (Offer Notice). An Offer Notice must state:
> >
> > > (a)   the purchase price for the Share Capital;
> > >
> > > (b)   the proposed settlement date (Settlement Date);
> > >
> > > (c)   the name of the Offeror; and
> > >
> > > (d)   any other terms of the offer.
>
> 1.2   Drag along
>
> > If a Shareholder (or Shareholders) holding not less than 75% of the total issued capital of the Company decide to accept the offer contained in the Offer Notice that Shareholder (or those Shareholders) may instruct the Company to give each other Shareholder notice (Drag Along Notice):

(a)   stating the decision of those Shareholders; and

(b)   requiring each other Shareholder to sell all their Shares to the Offeror on the terms contained in the Offer Notice at the same time as the Shareholders accepting the offer sell all of their Shares to the Offeror.

1.3   Obligation to complete

If the Company issues a Drag Along Notice to the Shareholders, each Shareholder must sell all of that Shareholder's Shares on the terms of the Offer Notice.

1.4   Settlement Date

On the Settlement Date:

(a)   each Shareholder must deliver to the Offeror title to all of its Shares free from Encumbrances;

(b)   the Company must receive on behalf of all Shareholders the total purchase price from the Offeror; and

(c)   the Company must account to the Shareholders for the total purchase price.

1.5   Limitations on warranties

A Shareholder will not be required to give any warranties on the sale of that Shareholder's Shares under this clause 1, except warranties that:

(a)   the Shareholder is the legal and beneficial owner of the Shares; and

(b)   the Shares are free from any security interest.

1.6   Attorney

Each Shareholder and the Company severally and irrevocably appoints any two Directors jointly as its agent and attorney with power to complete the sale as contemplated in this clause 1 (including the power for any two Directors together to execute all necessary documentation to complete the sale on behalf of that Shareholder or the Company (as the case may be)).

Veto Rights

Veto rights give the investor a right to prevent the company undertaking certain activities without the consent of the investor. Investors will often seek veto rights in the early stages of an investment. Obviously, the type of matters over which an investor should have a veto right at this stage of the investment cycle would be significantly less than the types of matters over which an investor may reasonably expect a veto at a much later stage of the investment cycle. The key items in respect of which we consider it to be appropriate to have veto rights at the early-stage in the investment cycle, include:

- payments to the founders / CEO of the company;
- transactions with related parties of the company; and
- changes to the nature and scope of activities of the company
- sale of the business and or key assets
- Issue of options or other related instruments

Information Requirements

This will generally entail specifications of information reporting to shareholders including annual reporting and monthly management financial reporting as may be desired.

Different stages require different agreements

There are four stages that companies progress through which could trigger changes to documentation of shareholder rights. Each of these approaches will reflect the quantum and stage of an investment. All too often, companies and investors take an approach that is not warranted and does not appropriately reflect the value of the company and the risk being taken by an investor. The approaches advocated are:

- **constitutional amendment** - generally used when only a small investment (under $50,000 for example) has been made and available funds do not justify seeking professional legal support;
- **shareholders' agreement (short form)** – used where relatively small investment has been made (under $250,000 for example) and where a legal professional has agreed that the approach will satisfy investor needs; and
- **shareholders' agreement (comprehensive and specifically negotiated)**.
- **mature company (IPO, merger, etc.)**

Stage 1: Constitutional Amendment

This approach is adopted when an investment is made at a very early stage of the company's life and the investment is small, less than $50,000 may be a guideline, however other considerations of the use of funds will also affect the decision to use this method. At this stage, the investor is taking a high technical risk but the dollar amount at risk is comparatively small. It is not in the company's or the investor's interest to spend excessive amounts on documenting the investment.

The approach involves amending the existing constitution to insert some key protection mechanisms commonly required by investors. These mechanisms may include veto rights and tag along rights.

Stage 2: Shareholders' agreement (short form)

A shareholders' agreement is a contract between all of the shareholders of the company and the company. It sets out how the company will be operated and the rights and obligations of the shareholders. The shareholders' agreement will override the constitution of the company, to the extent that the shareholders agreement is inconsistent with the constitution or deals with matters not dealt with in the constitution.

This is the recommended approach to be adopted for any relatively early stage investment with sufficient funds to approach legal counsel for a relatively simple, standard agreement.

Some of the key matters the shareholders may wish to see in the shareholders' agreement are:

- election of directors;
- drag along rights;
- veto rights;
- tag along rights; and
- information requirements.

Stage 3: Shareholders' agreement (long form)

Latter stage rounds of more substantial investment where the cost of the agreement is less important than the need to "get it right", will require the negotiation of a comprehensive shareholders' agreement specifically tailored to the particular transaction. There are no limits to the types of matters that the shareholders and investors may negotiate at this stage of investment.

In addition to the matters identified above, investors may seek:

- an alternative type of security (e.g. convertible note; preference share (possibly convertible and redeemable));
- greater range of veto rights / matters in respect to which there are special decision making rules;
- drag along rights (an ability to require the other shareholders to accept an offer for the purchase of all of the shares in the company);
- forced exit provisions (provisions that enable the investor to ensure that there is an exit event);
- down round protection (provisions that protect an investor if there is a share issue below the subscription price paid by the investor);
- compulsory sale of shares by shareholder for default of shareholders' agreement;
- control rights (allowing the investor to control the board / company if the company fails to meet key performance measures or is in danger of becoming insolvent).

Stage 4: Mature Company

If a company lists, matures or is taken over through trade sale or merger, then corporate law eventually becomes sufficient to satisfy minority shareholders. Shareholders' agreements can be removed when appropriate at this stage.

Preferred shares

Preferred shares provide another means for an incoming investor or group to take a control position in the board and potentially to develop a means to have an option to be the first to exit an opportunity. The preferences associated with these shares need to be clearly defined and understood. Most sophisticated angels will require some form of preference share.

Convertible Notes

A convertible note is a debt instrument often used when getting investment from angels. The advantage is that it is usually structured to defer the determination of the valuation of a company until others determine the valuation through some significant event. For example, if a venture capital round occurs in the future, the angel would have his investment converted at the same valuation as the venture capital. Since the angel has invested earlier and with increased risk, warrants are often included with the convertible note to provide the angel the opportunity to purchase additional shares at the same price at the time of conversion.

Simplicity of the Shareholder Agreement

The clauses within this chapter are very basic and much thought needs to be given to each individual case. Many clauses are standard and not included above. In general, a shareholders' agreement for a start-up venture should be no longer than 10 pages, however, many are often much larger than this.

Is a shareholder agreement required?

A shareholder agreement that protects all shareholders is extremely valuable. Many investors will not undertake investment without a shareholders' agreement. We've seen companies revisit shareholders agreements many times as new investment rounds eventuate.

We have also seen shareholders' agreements designed to remove the power of earlier investors and the founders for the purpose of exploiting the situation. Good legal advice is required by all involved in early-stage investment, however, during the earlier days, trust and openness, and simply documented agreements can serve entrepreneurs and angel investors well.

It is possible that a company can modify the constitution of the company to address some of the most basic elements of voting control. Many young companies have progressed well without a shareholders' agreement and/or changes to the constitution.

Investors will proceed without a shareholders' agreement if they believe the opportunity is well founded and the people involved are of good quality. Having a good shareholders' agreement protects all involved and is well worth the effort at the commencement of an investment in a start-up opportunity. With a well thought out shareholders' agreement in place, you should develop increased interest from angel investors.

17

Intellectual Property

Introduction

Innovation is critical to many companies in the present knowledge economy. Companies typically invest considerable time and money in creating new products and services, as well as in establishing a reputation. The system of intellectual property (IP) law aims to provide enforceable legal rights which deter others from copying or taking unfair advantage of the creative efforts or reputation of another.

Intellectual property rights (IPRs) can broadly be divided into two main areas: registered rights and unregistered rights.

- Registered rights are those which require the owner to apply to an appropriate authority for registration of those rights. The registration process may include an examination process to ensure that the rights should properly be granted. Examples of registered rights include patents, trademarks, registered designs, domain names and plant variety/breeders rights.
- Unregistered rights are automatic and so do not require an application for registration to be made. Examples of unregistered rights include copyright, design rights, rights under the law of passing off (which like trademarks deals with the protection of business good will and reputation) and the law of breach of confidence (which deals with the protection of confidential information, such as trade secrets).

It should also be noted that most, but not all, IPRs last for a fixed period of time. Patents for example have a term of 20 years from when a patent application is filed; registered designs have a term of 25 years; and copyright lasts for at least 50 years. By contrast, trade mark rights and trade secrets (such as the recipe for Coca-Cola®) can last indefinitely.

The process of investigating a company's IP also provides a mechanism to check that you are not infringing on others IP rights.

Protecting intellectual property through an IP portfolio

A company will typically rely on a mix of different IPRs. For example, whilst patents are a particularly strong form of monopoly right, in many cases trademarks are at least as important, if not more important. Trade secrets and confidentiality are especially important in the early stages of innovation since a company may not yet have had the opportunity to put patent protection in place. Registered designs and copyright protection also have an important role to play.

It is important that companies consider the whole range of IPRs when putting together an IP portfolio and not just focus on, for example, patents. Equally it is important to continue to develop the portfolio as the company grows and not just rely on a single piece of IP filed early on. When assessing a company's IP, investors should therefore look to see that the IP portfolio is appropriate for the stage of the company, is balanced and takes into consideration all possible forms of IPRs.

The importance of an IP strategy and managing risk

Good IP shouldn't be left to chance. Investors are, and should be, paying an increasing amount of attention to IP issues and the quality of a company's IP can be an important factor in whether an investor will decide to commit funds.

The younger a company is, the more its potential will be judged based on the IP portfolio, typically the patent portfolio, since other assets and turnover will generally be non-existent or negligible. A high quality IP portfolio can therefore have a crucial influence on the valuation of a company, the emphasis here, being on quality rather than simply quantity. A company's IP is not simply a list of assets: there must be a clear connection between its commercial objectives and the IP, as will be discussed in more detail below.

Accordingly, investors should be conducting some form of due diligence to determine what IP the company owns or has rights to use and the value of such IP.

Investors are used to dealing with the concept of risk and IP is simply another risk element to be taken into account in the overall deal.

Examples of IP risks

- The IP is not adequately protected
- The company does not have adequate systems in place to capture valuable IP, which is then inadvertently 'lost'
- The IP is not consistent with the business plan
- Expenditure is being made on IP that is not relevant to the business plan
- The company is pursuing an inappropriate filing strategy
- The IP is not valid
- The company does not own the IP (or does not have the right to commercialize in key areas, having licensed exclusively the technology to another party).
- The company's proposed commercial activities infringe on third party IP (i.e. there is no freedom to operate)
- The company is not free to use its chosen name or brand due to the existence of other trademarks. Changing a company's name and/or rebranding can be a very expensive exercise

In the case of technology-based companies, it has been common for only lip service to be given to conducting adequate IP due diligence. The highly complex nature of the technology assets and the extensive and highly technical nature of the due diligence process make it both time consuming and expensive. In addition, it is frequently done fairly late in the overall process when the investor is already leaning towards a positive decision to invest. As a result, despite the apparent importance of IP, the outcome of IP due diligence is rarely a deal breaker.

However, problems identified during IP due diligence can be, and have been, used to reduce the valuation of the IP, and hence the overall valuation. A loose analogy here is the process of buying a second-hand car. Provided that the potential buyer is happy with the car overall, minor defects will not necessarily cause the buyer to pull out of the deal, but the buyer will use them to knock the price down.

Accordingly, it is important for a company, prior to approaching investors, to have the proper procedures in place and to carry out internal due diligence to identify, and take steps to mitigate, IP risks. In this way, a company can ensure that it maximizes the value to investors of its IP portfolio and hence its valuation. From the perspective of the investor, problems encountered during the IP due diligence process may not only form the basis for a revised valuation but should also serve to generate an action list to remedy the deficiencies where possible and protect future investment.

The importance of an IP strategy

Studies in Europe indicate that companies with a formal IP strategy are more successful, on average, than those that do not, and also that a surprising number of companies do not actually have an IP strategy.

Companies should be able to demonstrate that they have an IP strategy in place that forms an integral part of the company's business plan. They should be able to demonstrate to investors why their IP is relevant to the company's commercial objectives and how it supports the business plan. Investors should ask companies to present their IP in the context of the business plan and not just as a list of IP assets.

What if the IP is not valid?

Typically, at the early funding rounds, the patent portfolio held by a start-up company will consist of one or more so-called provisional patent applications and perhaps pending international Patent Cooperation Treaty (PCT) applications. The prosecution of these applications will frequently be on a 'go slow' to defer significant patent costs.

However, pending patent applications are of lower value than granted patents since there is no guarantee that applications will ever lead to granted patents having commercially relevant claim scope. Where all the IP assets are pending patent applications and the company and the investors expect an exclusive position in the market once the patents are issued, it could be fatal to the business and the investment if no patents are granted.

The value of an unexamined patent application is very difficult to assess. One of the issues encountered during IP due diligence is that no so-called 'novelty search' has been conducted on new patent applications prior to, or during, the first year after a provisional application has been filed: there is therefore no evidence to suggest that the invention is patentable when it may be necessary to have this decision to support a decision to invest. One of the key questions that investors should ask therefore is whether a so-called 'novelty search' has been conducted.

A novelty search can provide an indication as to the "validity" of the patent claims and some assurance the patent will not easily be tossed out as unenforceable if (when) challenged. Investors are wise to consider this as a requirement of investment.

If no searches are performed, then the investment in the company may be the equivalent of buying a lottery ticket. This is because, without significant amounts of work being done, there is no way to assess the likelihood that any of the patents will be issued. Someone, somewhere else in the world may indeed be at the same stage or earlier in their development of an equal or better product.

A common approach in Australia is either to use commercial searching organizations or to commission the Australian Patent Office (APO) to carry out an international-type search after a provisional application has been filed. However, a useful alternative where the company plans to engage in significant commercial activity overseas, e.g. in the US and/or Europe, is to have the application searched by the European Patent Office (EPO) by filing a European patent application in the first instance. Arguably, the reputation of the EPO is such that a favorable search result carries more weight than a search carried out by the Australian Patent Office and at the very least is more indicative of likely success in Europe. A search carried out by a patent office, either the APO or the EPO, rather than by the company itself, also has the advantage of being an independent assessment.

With respect to trade marks, brand names etc. it is equally important that the company has established that it has freedom to use any such trademarks and brand names etc. since any changes at a later date can be very costly.

Do you have the freedom to operate?

A common misconception about IPRs, particularly patents, is that they give the holder the right to do what is specified in that right. However, IPRs are best viewed as negative rights: they are the right to stop others not a right to do it yourself. It is still possible that the right holder is stopped from doing what they want to do due to the existence of an earlier right (and in some cases a later right). It is therefore important for any company to establish its approach to managing the risk that other parties have IPRs that would prevent the company from engaging in its proposed commercial activities. The process of identifying third party IPR that poses a barrier to commercialization is usually termed a clearance search or a freedom-to-operate search. Such searches are typically very costly and therefore consideration should be given as to whether the risk of infringing someone else's IP justifies the costs of carrying out such a search. In addition, a clearance search is generally only conducted when there are concrete plans to commercialize a particular product or service. An alternative to a detailed clearance search is a 'clearance forecast' which seeks to map out in more general terms the IP landscape in a particular area to assist with identifying potential competitors and risk.

Innovation patent

(www.ipaustralia.gov.au/innovationpatent)
An innovation patent is a protection option specifically designed to protect inventions that do not meet the inventive threshold required for standard patents. It is a relatively fast, inexpensive protection option, lasting a maximum of eight years. Beware that an innovation patent will be issued without being examined. This means that you can secure an innovation patent on an invalid idea. However, a granted innovation patent cannot be enforced without having undergone a certification process conducted by the APO (which is essentially an examination

procedure to check that the patent complies with the requirements of the Patents Act). You, or a third party, can initiate the certification process, for which a fee is payable. This type of second tier patent protection is available in a number of other countries, where it is often termed a utility model.

In 2001, freelance patent lawyer John Keogh was issued with an Innovation Patent for a "circular transportation facilitation device", commonly called the wheel. Besides gaining international attention, he gave everyone an understanding that the innovation patent is a rubber stamp process requiring significant rigor to prove actual value.

Some 1000 innovation patents are registered each year in Australia. In general the value of an innovation patent relates to its validity within the Australian market only.

Managing the cost of IP protection

Obtaining registered IPRs in the form of granted patents and/or trademarks is costly. A separate patent or a trade mark must be obtained in every country where it is desired to obtain protection (with some exceptions such as the Community Trade Mark available in the European Union). For example, to obtain a granted patent in the US, Europe and Australia is likely to cost in the order of $100,000. It is therefore important that where costs are an issue, a suitable filing strategy is adopted to defer costs where possible and that IP portfolios are reviewed regularly to determine whether the IP is still relevant. The filing strategy should also indicate in which countries it is important to obtain protection to avoid wasteful filing of applications in countries that have only a small market for the relevant products or services.

A common strategy for deferring patent costs is to file an international application 12 months after the first provisional patent application. This defers the decision as to which countries to proceed in for a further 18 months. However, it should always be borne in mind that where the company is ready to commercialize early, or where there is a risk that competitors will enter the market early, that it may be desirable to secure registered IPRs quickly. There are, for example, various strategies for obtaining a patent grant fairly quickly, e.g. in less than 18 months from when the original provisional application was filed, where the commercial situation dictates.

A regular review of the IP portfolio and pruning of the portfolio where necessary is an important aspect of managing costs.

Where the IP is to be licensed out to other parties, this can assist with managed costs as the transaction could specify that the licensee make a contribution to the costs of securing IP protection.

Enforcement of Intellectual Property Rights (IPRs)

Intellectual property rights are of little value if they do not deter others from infringing those rights. However, litigation is expensive and diverts the attention and resources of key company staff from the important task of running the business. If the company is small and the competition is large, and aggressive, then initiating an action to enforce the company's rights may well be a daunting and challenging experience.

One strategy is to enter into alliances with larger partners who are more able to engage in enforcement of IPRs. Another strategy used successfully by IPR holders is to ensure that they set realistic license terms that make it more attractive for the other party, who also has to manage IP risks, to take a license than to risk litigation.

Since a party who is sued for infringement nearly always counter claims for invalidity of the relevant IP right, litigation also exposes the company to the risk of the loss of its IPRs. Accordingly, litigation should generally be seen as a last resort after other avenues of negotiation have failed.

It should also be noted that enforcement of IPRs in some foreign countries, particularly against local companies, can be especially difficult due to lack of judicial expertise in IP matters and/or corruption within the legal system. Even within countries with highly developed legal systems with specialist IP judges, success can vary significantly between countries and it is therefore important where possible to choose the best jurisdiction in which to start legal proceedings to maximize the chances of success (this is known as 'forum-shopping').

Summary

Investigation of IP protection strategies is essential to any early-stage venture. It can be complex and expensive but it does need attention early in early development of a venture. Weighing the pros and cons of timing, types of protection, geographic coverage and costs is difficult but done well may serve as a key element of a company's success.

Links for additional information are provided below:

US Patent & Trademark Office   www.uspto.gov
World IP Organization   www.wipo.int
European Patent Office   www.epo.org
United Kingdom IP Office   www.ipo.gov.uk
Google Patent Search   www.google.com/patents

18

Case Studies

Marketing French-made chardonnay to the British

Australian Mezzanine Investment Limited (AMIL) made 25 investments over 11 years. Three of these - two retail ventures and one agribusiness failed. Bill Ferris, a founding director of this company says that, "Good analysis in this business can minimize your losses, but for a tearaway success you have to be honest enough to say luck and timing are more important".

Joe Skrzynski, also a founding director of AMIL claims that each of the 65 entrepreneurs and staff of the 25 companies his company has backed in the past 11 years has seen the value of their share in their companies increase by at least $1 million. He says, *"Internal rates of return are cold and abstract figures. Identifying the number of millionaires we have helped to create is another way of measuring success."*

One of the successful businesses they backed was Cuppa Cup Wines which saw owner Robert Hesketh's original investment of $400,000 increase by 725 percent to $3.3 million when his company was taken over by Southcorp Wines.

The company purchased vineyards in the south of France, upgraded them and successfully marketed French-made chardonnay to the British market. Until then, French wines were marketed by region rather than grape variety.

Your idea is terrific, but ...

The time period from conception
to realization of some major innovations

	Conception	Realization	Incubation Interval (years)
Antibiotics	1910	1940	30
Automatic transmission	1930	1946	16
Ball point pen	1938	1945	7
Cellophane	1900	1912	12
Dry soup mixes	1943	1962	19
Frozen foods	1908	1923	15
Heart pacemaker	1928	1960	32
Instant coffee	1934	1956	22
Liquid shampoo	1950	1958	8
Nuclear energy	1919	1965	46
Nylon	1927	1939	12
Photography	1782	1838	56
Radar	1904	1939	35
Roll on deodorant	1948	1955	7
Self-winding Wristwatch	1923	1939	16
Television	1884	1947	63
Video tape recorder	1950	1956	6
Photo copying	1935	1950	15
Zipper	1883	1913	30

To achieve a 25 percent market penetration in the USA:
- **Household electricity took 46 years**
- **Telephones took 35 years**
- **Television took 26 years**
- **Personal computers took 15 years**
- **Mobile phones took 13 years**
- **While the internet achieved a 25 percent market penetration in just seven years!**

Rehearse and refine your presentation

Stephen Murphy and David Scallion are Melbourne based engineers who invented a quick-release binding for snow-boards to protect riders against injury. Their experience in locating and working with angels to assist with their project, included attending Investment Ready workshops in Melbourne. At the workshops they were required to make an oral presentation outlining their project

They attended a further eight workshops and made further presentations including the use of visual aids each time, becoming much more confident and proficient with their presentations each time.

They claim that their presentations became much more focused and to the point as a result of these rehearsals. A further benefit from these practice runs was a boost in their personal confidence, as well as reducing their original budget from $1 million to just $130,000.

They found that by selling the manufacturing rights after careful design of a prototype was a much better option than full on manufacturing. Their first presentation to a real investor was held in their home office. They made their by now well rehearsed and polished presentation, fielded the inevitable and necessary questions, and just a few weeks later had their angel.

Imax theatre

'Money will always back a good business entrepreneur rather than a great idea' The Imax theatre at Darling Harbor in Sydney is well known to both locals and tourists alike.

Few people realize however that its construction was funded in part by angels. Gary Blom the driving force behind the Imax theatre has experience in starting four companies and has worked as an investment banker in New York for 10 years. He originally planned to build the theatre and lease the Imax projector from the Darling Harbor Authority.

However, after approaching 74 investors with negative results he realized something was needed to act as a catalyst to ensure progress. It was only after Blom had contracted out construction of the $20 million theatre building that expressions of interest were received from four venture capital companies.

Obviously the money was important but Blom claims an investor with good contacts, political clout, the ability to assist in opening doors and someone who could bring him credibility were equally important.

Macquarie Investment Trust invested $3 million in the deal and later in conjunction with Blom's company, Cinema Plus, won 'the best early-stage category' in the Australian Venture Capital Awards.

Blom says that money will always back a good business entrepreneur rather than a great idea, a point reinforced elsewhere in this book.

Listening

Listening is a business skill which receives little recognition or attention. It is interesting to recount that we were born with two ears and just one mouth!

Many people, after meeting their angel, find it extremely difficult to listen to their angel and to heed their advice.

One of the further advantages of having an angel, apart from the finance they provide, is to have access to the business network and experience which most possess and bring with them. In our experience many people in business have their product manufactured by "... my mate. I have known him for years. Of course he gives me the best price!"

Despite the blind faith of these people in their 'mate', in most instances, substantial savings are made by having the product sourced from another supplier, often with quantum leaps in quality and design improvements. In one case a business had 'my mate' manufacture $100,000 worth of his dream product, which at the time met a market need, without getting any other quotations. "After all if my mate can't make it for the best price, who can?"

When the product failed to sell because of what potential customers perceived as a price that was too expensive, the businessman involved sought and found an angel to help in a rescue attempt of his business. At the very first meeting the angel suggested another manufacturer.

Strong protestations ensued with the business person claiming - as the angel had heard countless times in the past - that "... my mate makes the product., so it must be a good price."

A day or two later when the angel had obtained some other quotes which were up to 40 percent less than the current supplier, with superior trading terms - his 'mate' was called to defend himself and his pricing to his grim and white faced customer.

The person running the business was now faced with selling off his existing stock, for which he had paid far too much, at a loss, to match the prices from new suppliers if the business was going to proceed at all.

Careful analysis showed that his 'mate' supplier was paying up to 30 percent more for the raw material involved as well as other pricing problems and shortfalls due to outdated machinery and technology. In another case, a business-person with a very sound and later extremely successful, new patented invention found an angel to assist in the distribution of his product.

When the angel suggested a new supplier the same protests were aired. In due course however sanity prevailed and a new supplier cut the existing price by 60 percent and provided a vastly improved product incorporating new design improvements with superior and easier to machine materials.

An even worse case involved an entrepreneur who had his old employer - a very big Australian icon - manufacture his product, without bothering to obtain other quotations.

Similar conversations followed when his angel suggested an alternative supplier and once again the entrepreneur was faced with selling off his current stock at a deep discount and at a loss to enable the business to proceed and source product at a more attractive price.

The moral of these tales - entrepreneurs need to develop the ability to listen to their angels.

What are the ingredients for successful capital raising?

In a recent deal, $5 million was invested to obtain a minority shareholding in an Australian manufacturing company, by two well-known investment capitalists, together with a private group. The investment was expected to be in place for four to six years, with returns within three years.

It is interesting to record some of the things involved in making the deal which left an impression and aided the decision making process for both sides, the investors and the investee:

- The rapport
- The strength the investors would bring to the board
- The presence of a strong core-management team
- Skilful handling of marketing and key customers
- The potential of the company's expansion plan
- The experience of the existing CEO, both in Australia and abroad
- The current market and price leadership position of the company
- The skills and experience the investors would bring to the company, such as:
  - Corporate and merchant banking skills
  - Advice on acquisitions
  - A sounding board for recruitment issues
  - Assistance in raising more money, when required

Can you start with a PC and $20, and make millions?

Steve Outtrim did. Outtrim has received large amounts of press and media coverage in recent years as he floated his company Sausage Software, on the stock exchange in 1996.

For a few weeks in 1996 Outtrim, then just 23 years old, had a paper worth of almost $90 million as his internet company traded at around $1 after listing at 75 cents.

In 1998, Sausage Software shares had dropped to around just 15 cents. However during the second quarter of 1999 the shares had made a major recovery for several reasons, not the least being huge worldwide attention and interest in internet related stocks.

Some say it is the bureaucratic pressures that business attracts as it progresses through its growth phase.

Others point to a whole generation of computer entrepreneurs competing vigorously for the sales dollar.

Success secrets of tomorrow's stars

Some of the strategies that successful growth companies have used in their success, which came to our attention when researching this book, included:

- Outracing competitors to the market
- Helping customers do the same
- Selling product ideas to big customers before designing the product
- In one instance the customer bankrolled the supplier (acted as an angel), in order to have a secure source of product
- Avoid running out of cash
- Never turn down an order
- Buying all the components rather than trying to make them
- Leasing assembly plants
- Diversifying into closely related markets
- Using computer aided design (CAD) to shorten lead times
- Shortening delivery times

- Selling the machines to make the product, rather than the product
- Development of 24-hour hot lines for emergency service
- Establishment of R & D facilities in the actual target market area, such as Asia
- Relocating the business to be near the key customers
- Giving away the first of a new system to prove the concept and to have a working model available for demonstration to potential customers
- Benefiting from rising anxieties about the environment, by developing special chemicals and control devices to keep water systems free of small marine creatures, mineral deposits and corrosion

Graeme Wood

In 2000, businessman Graeme Wood asked himself, "What if (wotif) the online world could be turned into a new distribution channel for selling hotel rooms?" His company Wotif.com was the result and a recent BRW Rich List gives him a wealth of $251 million.

Wood says, "There were a lot of sceptics when we first went into business. A lot of people said it would never work. We've proved them wrong. There are two competing elements to my make-up - one, I am logical and insistent in technical terms, but on the other side, I'm not afraid of taking risks. I'd hate to die wondering. The internet is really an entrepreneur's dream. It broke all the rules so it let people who exploited the internet also break the rules."

Wood is a creative rule breaker. He took an idea about marketing discount accommodation online and made it work. In five years, his company has built an annual turnover of $350 million.

This former IT professional and one-time egg farmer has always preferred to work for himself. Competitive and driven by ideas, he admits to being easily bored. "I prefer to work for myself because I don't get on with bosses very well. I've got a very low boredom threshold. So If I can't do the interesting exciting things I want to do, I misbehave."

Wood says the entrepreneurial drive has always been there. "I can never remember a minute or a day in my life where I suddenly decided I would be entrepreneurial. It was something that just seemed to be there. I was the black sheep of the family."

The boy from Rockhampton has always felt a need to prove himself and says his zeal to create something new is a bigger motivation than money. He admits money has ebbed and flowed over the years. He spent 15 years in IT working for himself and also for big companies like IBM. He says the IBM philosophy of respect for the individual is one he's applied to his own businesses.

His stint as an egg farmer came during a downturn in the IT industry and saved him financially. It also taught Graeme about systems and allowed him to reinvent himself to get back into the IT industry.

The simple idea of using the internet to market last minute accommodation at a discount came in a moment of inspiration. "*There was a key moment when I sat down and thought about the whole idea and sort of sketched out a few things on a piece of paper and I could see it all come together. Well, I got up and paced around. I don't think I slept for two days.*"

In the beginning Wood didn't know what to do with the idea but he knew it was big. He approached his friend Andrew Brice, who decided to invest. "*I knew him to be enormously creative. In fact, I call him the rainmaker. He has this ability to conceptualize, with great ideas. And I recognized that ability and it was me who said to the other two guys, we should punt this guy."*

Getting investment money proved easier than getting the big hotel chains to come on board. *"When I started floating the idea to hoteliers, although the first reaction was very positive, some of them were very, very negative. Like they were rude, they'd just sort of throw you out of the office, effectively. But all that did was make me more determined to make it work."*

Wood persisted in selling the concept to enough hotels. But how would the market react? The first booking took two weeks to occur. A story five minutes before the evening news proved a turning point. To this day, word-of-mouth accounts for 80 percent of new customers.

There have been many imitators but not with the same success. Its growth in the past five years has been phenomenal.

Based in Brisbane, this international corporation has offices in five countries and more than 6000 accommodations on its books world-wide.

What makes an entrepreneur? According to Graeme Wood, *"entrepreneurship is really about taking risk. So if you're prepared to take the risk and wear the consequences of it, then that's fine. But I think there's a tendency for people to look for support to do it. They want to play with other people's money rather than their own and I don't think it really works that way."*

Wotif.com logs up to 100,000 bookings a month. This company which started with a wild idea floated on the Australian Stock Exchange in June 2006 at $2 per share and has since doubled to around $5. Wood received $42 million in the float and retains a stake worth $225 million.

What happens when exit strategies are not in place?

In August 1998 a high profile Australian cosmetic company made front page news and received wide media coverage when their angel decided to withdraw investment (reported to be $3.5 million).

The news of the problems with the angel were announced at a press conference at which sushi and champagne was served to those in attendance. The company's glamorous, and to many entrepreneurial types role model, CEO announced the problems and was most forthright in explaining the challenges and problems this would create.

The company was obviously faced with a lack of confidence in its ability to deal with its suppliers and a further confidence problem in trying to convince its retailers and distributors to continue their support.

Annual Business Angel Awards

Every year, winners of the Australian Business Angel Awards (ABAA) are announced by the Founders Forum and the Angels Institute in gala presentation. The event draws a national and international crowd making it a very interesting event. In his remarks when opening a recent conference, Richard Symon, the CEO, National Stock Exchange of Australia, was keen to talk about the activity of business development on the Gold Coast.

"In comparison, growing businesses on the Gold Coast out-paced other regions in Australia, like Sydney and Melbourne. There are a lot of entrepreneurial companies and a lot of talent on the Gold Coast.

These include entrepreneurial people and businesses, people who have made money, moved up here and who don't necessarily want to hang up there shingles and sit on the beach all day.

They want to combine the money they have made with the knowledge they have and be able to assist and involve themselves in other companies and new businesses. So in that regard they become mentor type investors. They don't necessarily want to just put their money into shares or into the bank to make interest.

What they want in fact is to get fantastic returns and direct involvement in growing these businesses. That is where the Founders Forum plays a part. A place where people meet and share ideas."

Winners of the Australian Business Angel Awards included Australian Biorefining who received the Australian Institute for Commercialization Most Innovative Investment Award.

What does award winning Australian Biorefining do?

Australian BioRefining is developing and commercializing new process technologies to use plant products as feedstocks for sustainable production. Their vision is clean sustainable production; "Green Chemistry" if you like. The company has developed a competitive process for the manufacture of gluconic acid using table sugar as a feedstock. They are also developing processes for competitively producing fructose, mannitol, and 2 keto-gluconic acid from table sugar.

As well as using sugar as a feedstock, the company is also investigating using cellulosic waste (bagasse) for manufacturing a range of food additives and industrial chemicals, as well as fly ash waste from sugar mill cogeneration plants to build environmental and agricultural remediation materials.

The company selects potential technologies for development based on the use of renewable resources and the potential to produce zero waste and pollution, and the economic potential of the technology. Their approach is to target profitable as well as environmentally sustainable technology development.

Buy low; sell high is the game to be played by angel investors, however, finding the company that will secure exceptional investment returns is not as easy as it seems.

The changing environment of venture investment

The phenomenal increase of new business growth is well documented.

Early-stage or angel investors are increasingly keen to grasp a piece of the next MySpace, Velcro, or Wotif.

Buy low; sell high is the game to be played by angel investors, however, finding the company that will secure exceptional investment returns is not as easy as it seems.

Buying low does not help the investor if the company fails after taking in and spending an angel investor's hard earned cash. Sloppy due-diligence practices and poor decision making by angel investors increases the risk to beyond where it should be.

Once angels are burnt, they tend to be very wary of investing again. The good news is that many changes are occurring in the industry that are reducing the risks associated with angel investment and it's important for you to know of these changes.

This book has shared with you how and why the dynamics are changing and how you can get a good opportunity funded and profitable.

The process of deal filtering and improved due-diligence is undergoing a transformation with programs including:

Matching services:

- BSI Capital and Investor Forum - Sydney, Brisbane and Melbourne
- Enterprise Angels - Brisbane
- Founders Forum - Newcastle, Gold Coast, Brisbane and Darwin

Entrepreneur support programs and networks:

- Australian Institute for Commercialization
- First Tuesday
- Information City
- OpenCoffee Club
- Triton Foundation
- Mentoring for Growth
- Mentoring for Investment

Angel groups and networks:

- Angels Institute - The national angel investment network
- Apollo 13 - Southeast Queensland
- AusFirst Angels - National - based on the Sunshine Coast
- Bio Angels - Adelaide
- Brisbane Angels - Brisbane
- Capital Angels - Canberra
- Strategon - National - based in Adelaide
- Victoria Investment Partners

Key government programs:

- COMET
- Commercial Ready
- R & D Tax Concessions
- Intermediary Access Program
- Enterprise Connect
- Global Opportunities (GO) Program
- Building Entrepreneur in Small Business

The majority of these programs and support mechanisms for investors and entrepreneurs did not exist 10 years ago. This is indeed, an industry in its infancy.

Much needs to be done to understand and maximize the benefit of early-stage/angel investment activities, and we will see huge growth in this area over the coming decade and therefore it is probably a good time to be an entrepreneur and an angel investor.

Kevin Fitzpatrick a part-time manager, accountant Andrew Brice and rural property manager Lyn Brazil invested in the WOTIF concept and within three years secured in excess of $100 million from the ASX float of WOTIF while retaining over 25 percent of ownership in the company.
This is the kind of investment return angel investors are seeking.

Crashes? What crashes?

The widely held belief that most start-ups fail in the first three years can finally be put to rest. An Australian Bureau of Statistics (ABS) survey reveals that MOST Australian businesses survive for at least the first three years.

As reported in BRW, after one year the survival rate of new entities was 92.3 percent. A year later, 88 percent were still operating. Of those that do "exit", the vast majority are non-employing or small-employing businesses.

In comparison growing businesses on the Gold Coast out-paced other regions in Australia, like Sydney and Melbourne. There are a lot of entrepreneurial companies here and a lot of talent on the Gold Coast.
Source: "Crashes? What Crashes?" Amanda Gome. BRW

Private Equity Invested in Fiscal Year 2006

In Australia, the largest amount of private equity invested was located in Victoria, which accounted for 24 percent of the total dollar amount, followed by New South Wales with a 22 percent share, and Queensland with a 15 percent share. However, New South Wales once again reflected by far the largest number of companies and rounds of financing, with a total of 56 and 62, respectively. New Zealand captured $736 million in private equity invested, or one-third of the total amount.

Private Equity Invested in Fiscal Year 2006		
	A$ Millions	Number of Companies Invested in
Consumer Related	1153	30
Other Products	433	55
Industrial/ Energy	201	23
Medical and Health	179	14
Biotechnology	129	10
Communications and Media	77	6
Computer Software and Services	30	18
Computer Hardware	30	2
Semiconductor/ Other Electronics	13	8
Internet Specific	6	8

At the end of June 2006, a total of $4.1 billion of new capital commitments was raised by private equity and venture capital funds. This level of new commitments effectively matches the record amount raised at the same time in 2005, and is well in excess of amounts raised in all other prior years. Successful fund-raising activity was dominated by buyout and other private equity funds. This compares with just $1.3 million in 1999.

At the end of June 2006, a total of $2.3 billion was invested by private equity and venture capital funds, reflecting growth of 20 percent over the $1.9 billion invested at the same time in 2005, and one of the highest dollar amounts on record. First-round investments once again led overall, accounting for 73 percent of the total amount. However, follow-on investments, or investments taking place subsequent to the first round, also increased significantly as compared to the year before.

Source: Thomson Financial & Australian Venture Capital Association Limited Survey, Fiscal Year Ended June 30, 2006

Conclusions

- A good angel or venture capitalist is ideally an experience rich, and capable business mentor, helping provide a new company with a market discipline, strategic direction, management expertise and useful introductions and access to other markets.
- A sizeable percentage of new companies backed by angels or venture capital will still fail despite their promising beginnings.
- A lot of angel and venture capital funds sit waiting for the right deal to come along. Appendices 3 and 4 provide contacts for support and funding.
- Always remember - everything is negotiable - and there is no such thing as a level playing field.

Acronyms

AAAI	Australian Association of Angel Investors
ABAA	Australian Business Angel Awards
ABN	Australian Business Number
ADI	Australian Distributed Incubator
ADR	Alternative Dispute Resolution
AIC	Australian Institute for Commercialization
AIM	Alternative Investments Market (UK based secondary exchange)
AIMI	Angels Institute Maturity Indicator
AISI	Angels Institute Success Indicator
AMIL	Australian Mezzanine Investment Limited
APTEX	Asia Pacific Technology Exchange
ASIC	Australian Securities and Investments Commission
ASX	Australian Stock Exchange
AVCAL	Australian Venture Capital Association
BIS	Business Information Service
BRW	Business Review Weekly
BSI	Business Strategies International
CHESS	Clearing House Electronic Subregister System
COMET	Commercializing Emerging Technologies
EDMG	Export Market Development Grants
EiR	Entrepreneurs in Residence
ESVCLP	Early Stage Venture Capital Limited Partnership
GST	Goods and Services Tax
ICA	Information City Australia
IIF	Innovation Investment Fund
IP	Intellectual Property
IPO	Initial Public Offering
IPR	Intellectual Property Rights
ISUS	Innovation Start-Up Scheme
IT	Internet Technology
KPI	Key Performance Indicator
M4G	Mentoring For Growth
M4I	Mentoring for Investment
MBI	Management Buy In
MBO	Management Buy Out
NASDAQ	National Association of Securities Dealers - Automated Quotations (US based secondary exchange)
NSX	National Stock Exchange of Australia (Australian small business exchange)

OMX	Nordic organization delivering key software for use in stock exchanges worldwide.
PBR	Plant Breeders Rights
PDF	Pooled Development Fund
PSF	Pre-Seed Fund (provided to improve private industry - access to University and Australian Government research agency research)
RBV	Resource Based View
REEF	Renewable Energy Equity Fund
SIM	Sustainable Investment Market
SME	Small and Medium (Business) Enterprises
SWOT	Strength Weaknesses, Opportunities and Threats
TFN	Tax File Number
USP	Unique Selling Point
VC	Venture Capitalist

Appendix 1 - "I've Been Everywhere" Lyrics

The success of the song "I've Been Everywhere", and it's 200 odd versions, has been nothing short of remarkable. Read why in this book in the chapter entitles "The Negotiation Process". "I've Got Spam in Here", one of many parodies is also listed here. Versions now include: "I've Had Everything", "I've Got Body Hair", "I've Seen Every Car", "Anyone But Bush", "We'll Campaign Everywhere Man", "I Ain't Goin' Nowhere"," I Hurt Everywhere", "I Know My Weed", "I've Done it Everywhere" plus many and some of over 100 language and country versions.

The US version of "I've Been Everywhere" written 1962 by Geoff Mack (Geoffrey Albert McElhinney)

I was totin' my pack
Along the dusty Winnemucca road
When along came a semi
With a high and canvas covered load
If you're going to Winnemucca, Mack
With me you can ride
So I climbed into the cab
And then I settled down inside
He asked me if I'd seen a road
With so much dust and sand
And I said,
Listen, Bud I've traveled every road in this here land

(Chorus)
I've been everywhere, man
I've been everywhere, man
'Cross the deserts bare, man
I've breathed the mountain air, man
Of travel, I've had my share, man
I've been everywhere

Been to Reno, Chicago, Fargo, Minnesota
Buffalo, Toronto, Winslow, Sarasota
Wichita, Tulsa, Ottawa, Oklahoma
Tampa, Panama, Mattawa, La Paloma
Bangor, Baltimore, Salvador, Amarillo
Tocopilla, Barranquilla, and Padilla, I'm a killer

(full lyrics at www.geoffmack.250x.com or go to www.youtube.com for many recorded versions plus parodies in video)

"I've Got Spam in Here"

The Piano Minstrel
Lyrics to the tune of I've Been Everywhere

I was checkin' my mail from what the trusty Windows browser showed
When along came a message 'bout a pill to get my manhood growed
If you're takin' me for a sucka then you'll have a surprise
And so I pressed the delete key but in another message flies
I ask you if you've got inbox with so much crap and spam
And I say, "Listen! I've gotten every mail that I can stand!"

I've got spam in here, man
I've got spam in here, man
Try me if you dare, man
I do not think it's fair, man
Of trouble I've had to bear, man
I've got spam in here

I'm getting:
Stock tips, and ski trips, thin hips, free computer
Paper clip, a toy ship, club strip, motor scooter
Bigger bra, coleslaw, how to draw, get a boner
Stay hard, credit card, bodyguard, not a loner
Bowflex, better sex, wooden decks, stony pillar
Where's my filter, hope will wilter, who's the guilter, I'm the biller

I've got spam in here, man
I've got spam in here, man
Sell me underwear, man
New products for my hair, man
Of phishing I've had a scare, man
I've got spam in here

I'm getting:
Weight loss, be your boss, use DOS, meet a rocker
Find old friends, sheep skins, clothes trends, here's a shocker:
Make it Big!, feed a pig, buy a rig, go to Vegas
soft porn, hard porn, kid porn, someone save us
this is free, this is free, scammin' me, it's all fake
was fake, will be fake, always fake, for God's sake!

I've got spam in here, man
I've got spam in here, man
Want a rocking chair, man?
I really do not care, man
Of hackers I've caught a pair, man
I've got spam in here

I'm getting:
Cancer pills, sex pills, Med pills, and camel fodder
Hair growth pills, tanning pills, cheaper thrills, holy water
Net games, hot dames, forward chains, what a bore
Hackysacks, thimbles, tacks, found a stack, so much more
I'm a hoe, make it grow!, a bigger weiner, it's obscener
Aquafina water cleaner, see what I mean?

I've got spam in here, man
I've got spam in here, man
Buy a wild mare, man
A coin that's very rare, man
Of tricksters that set up snares, man
I've got spam in here

I'm getting:
New wheels, ticket deals, higher heels, fix your body
Find some joy, sex toy, it's a ploy, let's get naughty
Give to me, all for free, security, social number
Business, with fake-ness, let's regress, I'm not dumber
How did you, get into, my address too, it's frustrating
They're waiting, and I'm hating, berating, aggravating

I've got spam in here, man
I've got spam in here, man
Makes me want to swear, man
I wish it wasn't there, man
I can't keep my inbox clear, man
I've got spam in here

I've got spam in here!

Appendix 2 –Confidentiality Agreement

The following sample confidentially agreement below has been used for over 15 years in both the US and Australia and has been signed by hundreds of investors including lawyers and accountants. It is provided as a sample only and the authors take no responsibility for its content or applicability to your venture. You are advised to seek legal advice when considering confidentiality issues for your venture.

[Company Name]

SAMPLE CONFIDENTIALITY AGREEMENT

THIS CONFIDENTIALITY AGREEMENT is made the .... day of .... 20___
BETWEEN the Recipient

....

AND [Company Name] [Address] [ABN], **Informant**

The Purpose of the disclosure is to enable the Recipient to evaluate and assess the potential of the business concepts described in the Confidential Information.

In consideration of the Informant having agreed to disclose the Confidential Information to the Recipient, the Recipient has agreed to accept the Confidential Information on the following terms covenants and conditions:

1   In this Agreement:
   a)   the expression "Informant" means the party which is disclosing Confidential Information and the expression "Recipient" means the party which is receiving Confidential Information;
   b)   "Confidential Information" means all unpatented inventions, ideas, know-how, concepts, trade secrets, processes, techniques, software, products and all other intellectual property, financial and business information and all other commercially valuable information of the Informant which the Informant regards as confidential to it and all copies, notes

and records and all related information generated by the Recipient based on or arising out of any such disclosure.

c)   Confidential Information excludes, or as the case requires, ceases to include information which is, or becomes:

(i)   available to the public in documentary form;

(ii)   at the date of its disclosure to the Recipient, already properly in the possession of the Recipient in written form otherwise than by prior confidential disclosure from the Informant;

(iii)   properly available to the Recipient from a third party having no obligation of confidentiality to the Informant;

(iv)   demonstrated by the Recipient to be independently developed by an employee or agent of the Recipient having no knowledge of such information the subject the disclosure.

2.   The Disclosing Party may disclose to the Recipient so much of its information, including Confidential Information as the Informant, in its sole discretion considers is necessary for the Purpose.

3.   The Recipient must:

(i)   keep all Confidential Information of the Informant confidential unless strictly required otherwise by law PROVIDED THAT where disclosure is required by law the Recipient undertakes immediately to notify the Informant of such actual or anticipated requirement and further undertakes to use its best endeavors to delay and withhold such disclosure until the Informant has had a reasonable opportunity to oppose such disclosure by lawful means;

(ii)   limit access to those of its employees, agents or confidential advisors reasonably requiring the Confidential Information on a strictly need to know basis for the purpose;

(iii)   not use the Confidential Information in any way which would be harmful to the best interests of the Informant;

(iv)   not use any Confidential Information in any way other than for the Purpose or as otherwise contemplated by this Agreement without the prior written permission of the Informant;

(v)   not copy, in whole or in part, any Confidential Information without the prior written permission of the Informant; and

(vi)   ensure that all employees, agents or confidential advisors to whom the Confidential Information is disclosed are legally bound under the terms and conditions or their employment agreements or otherwise:

• to keep the Confidential Information confidential;

• not to use the Confidential Information except for the Purpose.

4.   At any time upon the written request of the Informant, the Recipient must return to the Informant any documents originating from the Informant which embody Confidential Information and must not keep any copies in any form.

5. The Recipient obtains no proprietary rights of any kind to any Confidential Information as a result of a disclosure to it under this Agreement.

6. The obligations in this Agreement apply irrespective of the method of disclosure whether in writing, in computer software, orally, by demonstration, description, inspection or otherwise.

7. Each word, phrase, sentence and clause ("a provision") of this Agreement is severable and if a court determines that a provision is unenforceable, illegal or void, then the court may sever that provision without effecting the validity of the other provisions of this Agreement.

8. The Informant's failure to exercise or delay in exercising a right or power does not operate as a waiver of that right or power and does not preclude the future exercise of that right or power.

9. The law of this Agreement is the law of the State of [State]. The Parties submit themselves to the non-exclusive jurisdiction of the courts of [State] and courts of appeal therefrom.

10. The burden of showing that any Confidential Information is not subject to the obligation of confidentiality in this Agreement will rest on the Recipient.

SIGNED for and on behalf of the Recipient:
I/we agree to the above.

Signed: ....

Name: ....

Dated: ....

AND in the presence of:

Witness: ....

Name: ....

Index

www.ingramcontent.com/pod-product-compliance
Lightning Source LLC
Chambersburg PA
CBHW080549220326
41599CB00032B/6415